And The WORD Spoke Back To My Heart

Personal Vignettes From Selected Scriptures

Yvonne J. Miller

ISBN 978-1-64468-118-3 (Paperback)
ISBN 978-1-64468-119-0 (Digital)

All scriptures listed or referenced in this book come from the
King James Version unless otherwise stated.

Covenant Books, Inc.
11661 Hwy 707
Murrells Inlet, SC 29576
www.covenantbooks.com

CONTENTS

CHAPTER 1

And in the sixth month the angel Gabriel was sent from God unto a city of Galilee, named Nazareth,

To a virgin espoused to a man whose name was Joseph, of the house of David; and the virgin's name was Mary.

And the angel came in unto her, and said, Hail, thou art highly favored, the Lord is with thee: blessed art thou among women.

And when she saw him, she was troubled at his saying, and cast in her mind what manner of salutation this should be.

And the angel said unto her, Fear not, Mary: for thou hast found favor with God.

And, behold, thou shalt conceive in thy womb, and bring forth a son, and shalt call his name Jesus.

He shall be great, and shall be called the Son of the Highest: and the Lord God shall give unto him the throne of his father David:

And he shall reign over the house of Jacob for ever; and of his kingdom there shall be no end.

Then said Mary unto the angel, How shall this be, seeing I know not a man?

And the angel answered and said unto her, The Holy Ghost shall come upon thee, and the power of the Highest shall overshadow thee: therefore also that holy thing which shall be born of thee shall be called the Son of God.

And, behold, thy cousin Elisabeth, she hath also conceived a son in her old age: and this is the sixth month with her, who was called barren.

For with God nothing shall be impossible.

And Mary said, Behold the handmaid of the Lord; be it unto me according to thy word. And the angel departed from her.

—Luke 1:26–38

THE MOTHER

Mary was running with all her strength. She had been running until it seemed her legs would not be able to carry her any farther. So intent was she in her flight of escape, she was not even aware of the dust she was causing to stir and fall upon her damp face, the dirt collecting and mingling with the trickles of perspiration that coursed downward, streaking the skin of her face and neck. No, Mary was only aware of her immediate mission and plight which was to escape the noisy crowds of Jerusalem and be alone in her grief.

Her heart was near to bursting with grief, for only three days earlier had she witnessed from the foot of a cross her firstborn son, Jesus, cruelly crucified and put to death. It had not been a nightmarish dream from which she had been able to wake-up. No, it had been a reality. The horror of it all had replayed repeatedly, endlessly echoing within her mind for the past three days.

Reaching the outward limits of Jerusalem, she slowed her pace until she had to stop and gasp for great gulps of the crisp morning air, her heaving lungs screaming in agony, her body's physical strength having completely abandoned her. Bending down from the waist, she grasped her knees, struggling to keep her weary legs from collapsing.

Several minutes passed. With agonizing slowness, she straightened her body back to a fully upright position. Her breathing restored, her legs once again steady and stable, she renewed her quest to seek solitude and began to trudge the gentle, upward slope leading out of the city. On the stony and deserted road just outside of Jerusalem, she was a solitary and lone figure against the barren landscape.

Her broken heart was so heavily burdened and cumbersome that it seemed to weigh-down her very feet. She was oblivious to the early morning sun's rays that brightly shined down upon her countenance, exposing the smeared streaks upon her face, the swollen eyelids, and her red-rimmed eyes. The only immediate concern she had on this morning was in what she was feeling. For on this morning, coupled with her despair and grief, she was feeling unbelievably old.

Oh, how long ago it now seemed that she had once been a young handmaiden. A young girl with mighty hopes and dreams. However, scarcely anything had gone as she had then imagined or planned. Never would she have then believed that God would promise her the things he had, only to hurtle her into this darkest of moments. If this was a blessing, then what was a curse?

Questions of doubt and fear pummeled her mind. She had truly believed that God had given her his eternal, only begotten son. The Messiah. *His* Jesus.

Why then had God allowed this present darkness to come upon the lives of her and her son? How could he have forsaken them both in this way? Had she just mistakenly thought that she had heard from God from the very beginning? Everything she had believed that God had promised, had it all been just a lie in which she had believed?

Seeking to find some sort of reasoning in the midst of her despairing and grief-stricken heart, mind, and soul, she began to trace her thoughts back to the beginning. Back to the start of when she had very first believed.

* * *

All of her young life, as she was growing-up in Galilee, Mary had heard the reading of the book of the law from her Father, Heli. She had meditated day and night in its writings and had whole-heartedly observed to do all written therein.

When she had become a maiden of marriageable age, one particular portion of prophecy had caused her heart to stir every time she heard the words read aloud. Oh, how wondrously it had captured her attention! Written in the book of the prophet Isaiah, it spoke of a child that was to be born, the Messiah. He would also be known as Wonderful, Counselor, and Prince of Peace.

She remembered the day when hearing the words once again, a revelation had burst within her, striking as suddenly as a bolt of lightning. She had realized that *someone* would have to give birth to such a child...he would have to be born of a woman! When that revelation and realization flashed in her heart and mind, it had also ignited a spark within her spirit.

Who would be that woman? Who would the Lord choose to fulfill such a beautiful, wondrous prophecy? What young woman on earth would not want for such an honor?

Pondering upon the greatness of it all, she had boldly whispered a prayer of petition that she would be the woman chosen for that marvelous miracle. She had asked her God to bless her with the grace and favor of being the woman chosen to bear the child, the son, of which Isaiah the prophet had spoken. Never uttering a word of her petition to anyone else, so as to keep it close within her heart, she had then simply believed the Lord would grant her request.

It was shortly thereafter she had met Joseph, a just man, who was the son of Jacob. They had loved one another at first glance and soon they had become engaged. However, amid planning for a glorious wedding celebration, her purity of faith and belief had become shaken to its very foundation. It was during those plans that God chose to answer her petition, and it was not at all as she would have expected.

Her wedding ceremony plans paused in interruption when an angel of God, identifying himself as Gabriel, had appeared unto her declaring her blessed among all women. He had also told her of a creative act of God's Holy Spirit which was about to occur within her, causing her to conceive a child, the son of God. Gabriel had further instructed her that her cousin, Elisabeth, who had been barren all of her life and was now in her old age, had conceived a son also, and was already six months with child. After delivering such miraculous tidings, Gabriel had departed, leaving her awestruck and astounded. The Lord had heard and answered her prayer!

She had then gone immediately, in great haste and eagerness, to the city of Judah to visit Elisabeth, not even considering just how the promise from God would become fulfilled in her own life. She only knew in her heart that she had to get to Elisabeth!

Upon arriving at Elisabeth's house, they had eagerly shared one another's tales, both of whom joyously and expectantly talked of the wonders and mercy of God their Savior. Excitedly awaiting the birth of Elisabeth's child, Mary had stayed with Elisabeth for nearly three months. It was during this time she had discovered that she, herself, was with child. Moreover, without a husband! It was then that she had finally realized the enormity of her situation.

Whatever would Joseph think of her, or have to say concerning this serious matter?

Hastily, she returned to her home in Nazareth and found Joseph to tell him of her miracle. However, Joseph had not understood at all. Not at first. He had not seen or heard from her for almost three months since her startling disappearance. Though he loved her, he had not believed she could be pregnant without having been with another man. In fact, he had suggested divorcing her from their engagement contract, explaining to her that it seemed his only solution.

Mary had been devastated. Oh, he had been kind as he had spoken with her of his final decision, willing to have the divorcement performed in private, not desiring to participate in publicly shaming her. Nevertheless, his kindness had not prevented the hurt Joseph had caused Mary by not believing she had not been with another man. Joseph had not believed Mary's pregnancy to be the miracle she was claiming.

It had taken an intervention of the angel Gabriel once again, to explain to Joseph and save the situation, confirming that none other than God's Holy Spirit had indeed, conceived Mary's child. She and Joseph had thus been married after all, although in haste, and her wonderful son, Jesus, had been born. He had grown, becoming strong in spirit and filled with the wisdom and grace of God.

What a precious joy her firstborn son had been to her! As Jesus had grown into young adulthood, she and Joseph had both been astonished at the love their son had for God's word. As he had continued to increase in stature, they had also noticed that Jesus continually found favor with both God and man. What a blessing he had been!

She had continually marveled at his very existence, pondering upon the additional things spoken to her in the past about Jesus. How, according to prophecy, he was the Son of the Highest and in him, the government would rest upon his shoulders and whose peace would be eternal. Additionally, Jesus would one day sit on the throne of David and reign over the house of Jacob forever.

Reminiscing and marveling now upon those past promises of her young son's greatness and goodness, she suddenly remembered the time when he had been twelve-years-old, and she and Joseph stricken with fear and grief had thought they had literally lost their son, Jesus.

They had traveled by caravan to Jerusalem to attend the traditional Feast of the Passover, as they had done faithfully every year of their lives. After fulfilling the Feast of the Passover, they began the journey to return home. Having traveled with the caravan an entire day and stopping for the evening, she and Joseph had then discovered Jesus was not in their company of kindred. Searching the entire population of the vast caravan, to no avail, the next morning they had traveled in return to Jerusalem. It was not until the third day of their return journey that they had discovered his whereabouts.

They had found him in the Temple, sitting in the midst of the temple teachers. He had been both listening to the teachers of the laws of God, and questioning them, astonishing everyone present with his seriousness, discernment, and knowledge of the Holy Scriptures.

Mary and Joseph, upon espying Jesus, oblivious to their surroundings, had both rushed to him, calling out his name, the panic they had been experiencing the last three days still fresh in their hearts and minds. Mary had reached him first, throwing her arms gratefully around his youthful body, clutching him closely to her pounding heart.

When the joy of finding him in safety had subsided, and reason had settled in, without hesitation, letting him know with certainty what she and Joseph had just been through, Mary had then openly chastised her son. Oh, how could he have done this to them and have been so thoughtless, she had emotionally asked of her son, her voice choking with a bridled sob. Surely, he must have known the terror they had experienced as parents for these last three days, thinking him lost or worse still, kidnapped, or even killed!

Mary and Joseph were then both bewildered at their son's response and his calm demeanor. She remembered the innocence in his voice as he had gazed-up at their worried expressions with puzzlement, asking her why were they so worried about thinking him lost, or why had they not known without a doubt where they could find him? Did they not know he must be about his Father's business?

That boy! A tiny smile tugged at her heart in her remembrance of that day.

Actually, that one particular incident had been the only time in which she and Joseph had ever experienced any form of behavior from their son that had caused them to trouble or sorrow. For the remainder of their son's life, Mary reflected, he had never again caused them one bit of worry. He had been the perfect son and the joy of their lives.

As she stood now, recalling the past, alone in the middle of a deserted road, reality once again reminded her that her perfect son, the joy of her life, was this time, indeed, gone. This time truly lost to her, his battered body dead and lifeless, enclosed within a tomb. How was she to continue going on with her life, a life void of her precious son?

The enormity of the situation overcame her. Anguish crashed down upon her, consuming her totally. Anguish so extreme, it was as if a sword pierced through her very soul.

Broken in spirit and overwhelmed, she dropped to her prayer-worn, calloused knees upon the dusty Jerusalem road, clasping her hands tightly together. She turned her tormented spirit and face upward, imploring the pale blue sky of the immense heavens, still seeking an answer in the only way she had ever known.

Suddenly, there shined round about her a brilliance of shimmering light. It overshadowed her, immersing and wrapping her safely in a blanket of pure love. She closed her eyes, wanting to focus only on this gift bestowed upon her. Peace began embracing her heart, mind, body, and spirit and it was unlike anything she had ever before experienced, a peace beyond any comprehension or understanding. It flowed through her every fiber as it began, ever so gently, to remove the sword of anguish from within her tortured heart, tenderly binding-up her broken heart and wounded spirit and soul.

Then it happened. The answer. The only answer she would ever need. She heard the answer in a still, small voice that spoke to her heart. A voice she recognized instantly as only a Mother's heart could. She heard the truth, once again, of her son's words, spoken gently but firmly, a knowing smile of complete understanding lighting her countenance. Causing her to believe. Once again.

Mother, Mother! Surely, you must know that I am about my Father's business!

* * *

And blessed is she that believed: for there shall be a performance of those things which were told her from the Lord.[1]

---
[1] Luke 1:45

CHAPTER 2

And it came to pass in those days, that there went out a decree from Caesar Augustus, that all the world should be taxed.

(And this taxing was first made when Cyrenius was governor of Syria.)

And all went to be taxed, every one into his own city.

And Joseph also went up from Galilee, out of the city of Nazareth, into Judaea, unto the city of David, which is called Bethlehem; (because he was of the house and lineage of David:)

To be taxed with Mary his espoused wife, being great with child.

And so it was, that, while they were there, the days were accomplished that she should be delivered.

And she brought forth her firstborn son, and wrapped him in swaddling clothes, and laid him in a manger; because there was no room for them in the inn.

And there were in the same country shepherds abiding in the field, keeping watch over their flock by night.

And, lo, the angel of the Lord came upon them, and the glory of the Lord shone round about them: and they were sore afraid.

And the angel said unto them, Fear not: for, behold, I bring you good tidings of great joy, which shall be to all people.

For unto you is born this day in the city of David a Saviour, which is Christ the Lord.

And this shall be a sign unto you: Ye shall find the babe wrapped in swaddling clothes, lying in a manger.

And suddenly there was with the angel a multitude of the heavenly host praising God, and saying,

Glory to God in the highest, and on earth peace, good will toward men.

—Luke 2:1–14

THE FATHER

A vast host of angels gathered round about the outside perimeter of the heavenly throne room. The gilded door leading to the inner courtly chamber was ajar, but not one of the angels moved a wing to approach nearer or to attempt to peer within the sacred inner chamber. They all knew, in due time, the Father would inform them as to why he had summoned them.

The entire heavenly atmosphere charged and tingled with expectation. Whatever the reason for their summons, the angels whispered amongst themselves, it was bound to be glorious. For they could not help remembering the last time they had all assembled like this. On that long-ago day, they had witnessed in awe the cornerstone and foundations of the earth laid and fastened by their Father, the Lord himself. That day, viewing the magnificent splendor of the Father's handiwork, so filled with wonder, in spontaneous unison, they had collectively burst into song, singing and shouting their applause.

That was why now, curiously and wonderingly, they questioned between themselves what it could be this time. One thing was certain. There was never a dull moment in the Father's sanctuary. What a calling!

Meanwhile, within the regal throne room of the sanctuary's courtly inner chamber, beneath an iridescent, emerald rainbow, the kingly throne was temporarily unoccupied, its footstool purposely pushed aside. The royal throne's usual occupant, the Father, was much too excited to be sitting calmly reposing upon the throne at such a time as this.

Instead, he was briskly pacing back and forth, his footsteps echoing upon the crystal-sea-of-glass floor. He had waited so very long for this momentous occasion. Now that it neared, he was experiencing emotions he had never before encountered. His only begotten son was about to be born!

The Father had many other sons in whom he delighted and loved very much. As a matter of fact, two-thirds of those sons, summoned and gathered just outside his door in the outer sanctuary, were now faithfully awaiting further instructions from him. These sons devotedly doted upon him and had always served him with unflinching loyalty. He was extremely proud of them, more than honored to have them as sons.

However, this son, whose birth he was now awaiting, was to be unlike any other son he had ever before had. This son would be the Father's first, and only, to be born of a woman.

Such a birth had never before taken place. Even this child's name was to be different from any other name. The Father had carefully chosen this son's earthly name, Jesus; a name whose meaning was Savior. For only this son would be able to save and redeem mankind, the Father's earthly creations, from their fallen condition. Sin.

All those now gathered within the outer perimeter of his courtly chamber had known, from the beginning, there was an appointed time for the only begotten son's birth and appearance. So should he now inform them that the long-awaited anticipated birth was imminent?

The Father decided to look in upon the earthly scene just one more time before he did so. Briskly walking over to the throne room's great, eastern window, he raised its opulent, green jade frame. Leaning upon the window's cool, smooth sill, he gazed down upon the earthly town of Bethlehem, the chosen site for the birth of his only begotten son. Darkness blanketed the sleepy little town, but a newly lighted star that he, himself, had previously lit, aided in his viewing. It was a star so brightly lit, it was the brightest star of the eastern sky.

The Father, able to see every minute detail, eagerly focused his sight upon a lowly manger in Bethlehem. The manger was the feeding trough of a stable, intended for the use of only camels and horses.

However, in the midst of the manger, surrounded by various live-stock, lay sweet little Mary, the young woman in whom the Father had found favor, and had chosen to bear his only begotten son.

For the moment, she lay restlessly, propped up on a bed of hay covered with a rough woolen blanket. Joseph had hurriedly fashioned the makeshift resting place for her only hours before. He'd had to do so because for many long hours previously throughout the day, Mary had been experiencing labor pains, and had been in desperate need of a resting place.

Joseph and Mary had arrived into Bethlehem just this night after traveling, with much trepidation due to Mary's pregnancy, from their hometown of Nazareth. They had made the long, arduous journey only in obedience to a newly ordered Roman decree issued by the reigning Caesar Augustus that every citizen was to travel to specific government-appointed cities in order to pay taxes. Joseph was of the house and lineage of David. Therefore, the requirement was he had to journey to the city of Bethlehem. The town's only inn had not been able to accommodate Mary and Joseph upon their arrival. The inn had already filled beyond capacity with the earlier arrival of the many migrant taxpayers. The manger had been the only other accommodation available.

As the Father lovingly continued to look upon this scene in Bethlehem, he noticed Mary's face begin to grimace with discomfort. It quickly became evident she was experiencing another hard labor pain. Beads of perspiration lined her brow. Although she spoke not a word as she steadfastly endured the pang of childbirth, she sensed the actual birth of her child had to be very near. Mary silently breathed a prayer of petition for the strength she needed to deliver the son of promise.

The Father, instantly responding, whispered a thought into Joseph's heart. In answer, Joseph grabbed a hollowed-out, wooden bowl from the few meager belongings they had brought along for their journey, and quickly dipped it into another trough of cool water that was close by. Turning around and quickly kneeling at Mary's side, he held the bowl up to Mary's dry, parched lips. Mary gratefully took a sip of the refreshing water before leaning back her head and closing her eyes in momentary respite. Soaking the edge of one long, loose sleeve of his outer coat with the remaining water in the bowl, Joseph then began gently dabbing at his wife's perspiring face, wishing there was more he could do to help her.

This was their first child, and being young and newly wedded, they had no experience in such matters. Alone and also away from home was not helping the situation at the moment. However, they were both thankful they at least had found somewhere for Mary to rest and give birth. The bond of love between them had enabled them to make this journey very dependent on the Lord, and each other. They were still trusting the Lord would provide their every need and direct their every step.

Joseph, now keeping a watchful eye upon Mary's resting face, waiting for any sign of the next wave of discomfort he knew was soon to come, suddenly and inexpressibly found himself overcome with an overwhelming rush of love for his young bride. Briefly, he leaned over and tenderly kissed his young wife's cheek.

Bless you, Joseph, the Father silently thought to himself. The Father's trust in Joseph, coupled with his trust in Mary, was complete. They both had relied upon him to take care of them, and not once had he been disappointed in either of them. When their life's journey ended, neither would they be disappointed in him. The Father had already prepared special rewards for them both. Nevertheless, that remained in the future.

The Father's thoughts quickly became interrupted when another spasm of childbirth gripped hard within Mary, causing her to call out to him. There was now hardly any relief between the surging waves of her labor pains. The Father could barely contain his compassion for her, and unknowingly leaned a little farther from his window, silently coaching from afar, *Push, Mary! Push!*

Immediately, Joseph's voice gave words to the Father's thoughts as he encouraged his wife to push with the pain. Mary gritted her teeth as she simultaneously clenched her hands into tight little fists, causing her knuckles to gleam whitely beneath the olive-toned skin. She closed her eyes to concentrate upon pushing with all of her might. The pain was almost more than she could bear. *Surely the time to deliver my son must be near!*

As quickly as the thought raced through her mind, the continuing pain began to crescendo into one great final spasm before releasing her. Inundated with relief, Mary allowed her exhausted body to relax. As a peaceful calm swept over her, in the distance, she could hear a sound with which she was quite unfamiliar. *Why, it is Joseph… he is both crying and laughing in the same breath!*

A small, loud cry began to mingle with Joseph's cry. Mary's tired eyes flew open. As they did so, Mary saw, by the light of the brightest single star she had ever beheld, her husband, Joseph, holding in his arms the tiny newly-born son. Jesus.

Still viewing from far above, the Father also wept unashamedly with joy and pride. As he watched Mary stretch out her arms to enfold the babe and hold him close to her heart, the Father's tears of joy and pride quickly became tears of aching sadness, his own arms longing to hold and touch, if only for just the briefest of moments, the only man-child he would ever have.

Yet in his omnipotence, he knew if he ever reached out and physically touched his child, if even for the breath of a second, he would never be able to let him go. And this he could not allow. His long-ago plan for all mankind's eternal redemption he had imparted into the coming of this one-and-only son's existence. Therefore, as the tears streamed down his face, the Father had no other choice but to be an observer only.

Finding the only other way in which he could participate at this moment in his son's birth, even though the Father knew he had perfectly formed and fashioned his son, he shared his thoughts with both Mary and Joseph. *Count his little toes and fingers. Just for the sheer joy of their being so tiny, yet so complete.*

The Father's thoughts became Mary and Joseph's thoughts as they adoringly inspected and counted all ten little fingers and ten little toes. They were in awe of just how perfectly formed they were.

Delighted, the Father again breathed another thought into their hearts. *Did you notice he is such a beautiful boy? Or notice even his hair is beautiful and perfect?*

The Father observed as Mary and Joseph took turns boasting to one another in hushed and reverent tones surely this must be the most beautiful baby ever born on earth. Why, even his hair was perfect! Was it not sweet how it now damply curled ever so slightly upon his head?

Knowing his son was the very image of himself, with a lump in his throat, the Father could not resist one last whispered round of thoughts. *Observe how very blue his eyes are. Have you ever seen such a color of blue? Who do you suppose he looks the most like?*

As she began delicately binding her newborn son snugly in swaddling clothes, Mary felt Joseph's enraptured gaze upon her and her son as he knelt beside them. She felt a tug within her heart, her thoughts momentarily distracted. *My sweet Joseph! He has been so good to me. Even though this child is not his own, obeying the Father's instructions, he still took me to be his wife. Joseph has not even so much as uttered a harsh word to me since. He has remained faithfully and truly devoted to me.*

As she cradled her now fully swaddled infant son within her arms, only his eyes now visible, Mary lovingly gazed into her precious son's beautifully blue eyes. Mary's heart experienced an instant inspiration.

Looking up to beam a radiant smile at Joseph, she excitedly declared, "Joseph, have you noticed his eyes are blue, just like yours? What person will not say our son has definitely taken after your side of the family by having the same beautifully blue eyes as you!"

Joseph gave her a quizzical look for a long moment. Finally, understanding lit upon his face. Smiling broadly, Joseph's chest swelled out like a proud peacock with outstretched tail feathers! Mary could not help but laugh aloud at the sight.

However, in the throne room, the Father's heart felt as if it would break with sorrow. Desolately, he kept his next thoughts contained solely within his own heart. *No, Mary, he has __my__ eyes. My son is the mirror image of myself. When you see him, you see __me__. The Father. And it will always be so. However, for now, I must leave it alone.*

Forcing his eyes and thoughts away from all sentimentality, the Father compelled himself once again to return to the joy of the occasion. And as he did, elation replaced the dull ache in his heart. *Behold! My only begotten son has been born! Surely there must be someone else with whom I can share the good news.*

Wonder of wonders! He had totally forgotten about the angels he had summoned earlier. *Gracious goodness! What is the matter with me? I have to get moving!*

Hurriedly pulling his head back inside the eastern window of his courtly chamber, he inadvertently bumped it on the window's frame. It did not hurt him a bit but rattled the window's crystal glass panes, the sound resonating throughout the great throne room. However, it did muss-up his neatly groomed snow-white hair, causing several bunches to stick out prominently.

Running hastily through the inner sanctuary, he headed straight for the gilded door he had left ajar, skidding across the slippery, crystal-sea-of-glass floor. Grabbing for the door's edge, he flung it wide open, catching the gathered angels outside totally by surprise. There was a colossal whoosh of fluttering wings as a startled multitude of gathered angels turned to face him.

And what a sight it was they beheld! There stood the Father, feet spread widely apart to catch his balance, his hair all askew, and his long, white, stately robe billowing around his feet. What, in heaven's name, had he been doing?

His balance restored, throwing a glance over his shoulder at them, the Father rushed past, exclaiming, "Come on boys, there is great joy to behold and proclaim! Meet me in the city of David. I have just witnessed the birth of Jesus. My only begotten son has arrived, the Savior of the world, Christ the Lord!"

With the Father riding upon the wings of the wind, the angels followed closely behind. Using the brightly lit eastern star as a landmark and guide, it took just seconds to arrive at their destination.

As the vast host of angels expectantly hovered in the heavens just above the fields of the outskirts of Bethlehem, only one pre-appointed angel alighted upon the ground. A group of shepherds, groggily attempting to remain awake as they kept watch over their flock by night, occupied the field with him. With the Father concealed directly behind him, the solitary angel made visible his own appearance, his presence radiating so gloriously it nearly blinded the abiding shepherds.

No longer half asleep, the shepherds gasped with fright. Due to the brilliantly emanating light, all they were able to see was the outline of the enormous angel who stood towering above them. To say the shepherds were mightily frightened was an understatement. They were absolutely terrified!

Observing their collective terror, the angel promptly stated to the shepherds not to be fearful. For he was there only to proclaim good news of great joy. This day, unto all mankind, in the town of Bethlehem, a deliverer had been born, Christ the Lord. As a sign of confirmation, the shepherds would find the newly-born infant lying in a manger, wrapped in swaddling clothes.

As the pre-appointed angel completed his proclamation, the remaining angels suddenly appeared also, the heavens filled with their visible presence. With incredible joy, in unison, the vast host of angels burst into singing and shouting their applause, proclaiming, "Glory to God in the Highest, and on earth peace, good will toward men."[2]

While the angels were shouting their praises, the Father quietly slipped away. There was one last thing he wanted to do before he departed. Before the shepherds arrived to view for themselves the event just made known unto them, the Father wanted to have a moment, alone, with his son.

Wrapping a cloud around himself so the brightness of his glory would not disturb anyone, he quietly tiptoed to the manger temporarily housing Mary, Joseph, and Jesus. As he came upon the manger, sensing his presence, the huddled livestock turned to look, their soft brown eyes curiously watching as he made his way toward them. They silently parted, giving reverence to their master and creator.

Standing upon the very earth he himself had spoken into existence, the Father gazed for the last time at the scene before him. An exhausted Mary and Joseph lay sleeping soundly upon the bed of hay, with Jesus nestled closely in between them, wrapped snugly in his

---

[2] Luke 2:14

swaddling clothes. Mary and Joseph each had an arm lightly crossed over the baby, as if to shield him from all harm. Just as the Father had purposed it should be.

Although his son would never feel the physical warmth and loving touch of his heavenly Father's own everlasting arms, the Father would make certain not even a hair on his son's head would suffer harm unless appointed.

Only in the future of his manhood would the appointed time arrive when this son would willingly lay down his life, as a lamb led to the slaughter, to fulfill the Father's plan of redemption for all mankind. With the Father's great love then made manifest through this son's life and sacrificial death, the world would only then come to know that both the Father and the son's love, indeed, was genuine and complete.

Tears welled up once again in the Father's eyes as he remained gazing upon the miracle of this, his tiny son. Slowly, the sleeping infant's eyes opened. For one brief moment in eternity, blue eyes looked into blue eyes and fastened securely, locked forever in boundless love.

The moment passing, the infant Jesus yawned and returned to peaceful sleep. The Father, walking on air, arose to join the heavenly host of angels as they were ascending heavenward. Once again catching the wings of the wind, the Father and angels vanished into the night.

Only two things remained as evidence of the Father's visit and the Father's love toward all men. The night's brightly lit eastern star. And the light of the world, his newly-born son, Jesus.

* * *

For God so loved the world, that he gave his only begotten Son, that whosoever believeth in him should not perish, but have everlasting life. For God sent not his Son into the world to condemn the world, but that the world through him might be saved.[3]

---
[3] John 3:16–17

CHAPTER 3

And he went out from thence, and came into his own country; and his disciples follow him.

And when the Sabbath day was come, he began to teach in the synagogue: and many hearing him were astonished, saying, From whence hath this man these things? And what wisdom is this which is given unto him, that even such mighty works are wrought by his hands?

Is not this the carpenter, the son of Mary, the brother of James, and Joses, and of Juda, and Simon? and are not his sisters here with us? And they were offended at him.

—Mark 6:1–3

THE CARPENTER

Jesus, the carpenter, finishing a long day's hard work, is preparing to close up his workshop. A gentle breeze carries the sound of a solitary cricket's loud chirping, and with night approaching, a chill is in the desert air.

The carpenter carefully lights the flaxen wick of a clay oil lamp protruding from the single-story, rough fieldstone wall so he can better see to sweep up the workday's accumulation of curled wood shavings and coarse sawdust covering the hard-packed clay floor. Reaching behind the open, pivoted door, he grabs a straw broom to begin the task of sweeping the shavings and sawdust into one mounded pile.

As he does so, abruptly, a brief recollection first flickers, then flames into his thoughts. His thoughts now flip backward to another time, another place, covered with another mounded pile of a different sort.

Earth's dust.

The time was in the beginning. The place was a land named Eden, a paradise on earth. It was the sixth day of creation. On this sixth day, he and the Father had just fashioned and created from a mounded pile of dust, the first Adam. They had created him after their own image. Overhead, a pure white dove fluttered in the air. The newly formed sun beamed its bright rays down upon their creative workmanship.

There lay Adam, flat on his back, arms outstretched. He was beautiful to behold, yet lifeless. There remained only one final act to complete him. He and the Father looked at each other and smiled, knowing and possessing all needed for the completion. Pure excitement, mingled with high anticipation, mounted as their creation of love was about to receive their crowning touch.

In perfect harmony, both he and the Father inhaled deeply. Their lungs filled, then overflowed. The overflow filled their cheeks, causing them to balloon outward. Eyes sparkling, he and the Father, as one, both exuberantly exhaled and breathed into Adam's nostrils the breath of life. Adam became a living soul. The Father grabbed Adam's left arm, he grabbed Adam's right arm, and together they joyfully lifted Adam up onto his feet. Their job is complete. He and the Father both agreed. It had been the most rewarding day's work.

With the carpenter's thoughts returning to the present, he realizes he cannot see very well due to the warm tears that have gathered in his misted, blue eyes. Halting the sweeping temporarily of the shop's refuse, using an edge of one of the long sleeves of his seamless, linen robe, he wipes away the tears which have now splashed downward onto his bearded face. Through the ages, he, the last Adam, has lost count of all the tears that he has shed over the first Adam, and all the others in between. But now is not the time to reminisce. There still remains work to complete in preparation of closing his shop to end the day's work.

He methodically resumes sweeping the wooden remnants upon his workshop's floor. Upon finishing the task, he scrapes the great heap of wood refuse onto a large, thin scrap of wood, tosses it all into a nearby barrel, and places the workshop's broom back behind the open door.

His dusty, sandaled feet now quietly, with confidence, carry him to a dim, far corner of the shop. In preparation for tomorrow's commissioned job, his rough, calloused hands lovingly select a plank of stacked cedar wood from the small assortment of his shop's meager supply. As he carries the aromatic plank to his workbench at the back of the shop, his eyes draw to the large, wooden, pegged shelf on the wall he now views in front of him. Wedged between two pegs, the iron from his work hammer catches a dancing ray from the lighted lamp. Atop the dusty, pegged shelf, three six-inch rusted nails lay scattered, casting eerie shadows upon the thinly plastered wall. Earlier in the day, while searching his shop for various materials needed for a previously commissioned job, he had put aside the discarded nails after discovering them not fit for use.

This scene triggers a second vision to image within his mind. The new vision plunges him forward in time to another job in which he commissioned to do, only in a much different workshop. However, it too will require the same tools of his trade; wood, nails, hammer.

And dust.

The dust of Golgotha's hill.

Blinking in effort to clear his mind of this future image, the carpenter is able, momentarily, to return again to the present. He casts his glance at the now flickering lamp. Its wick, made of old swaddling cloth soaked in olive oil, is beginning to smolder, almost ready to burn-out. A vision of the past now merges with a vision of the future. The past recalls an infant's back, wrapped in swaddling clothes, placed onto the roughly hewn wood of a manger. The future projects a man's bared back; flesh mangled and tattered, placed onto the splintered wood of a Golgotha cross.

The carpenter's back involuntarily stiffens. A gasp escapes from him as this last, future scene propels him onward. Instead of the darkened room of a carpenter's shop, all he can now see is the darkened sky of Golgotha's hill. He is flat on his back, arms outstretched, and a rugged cross underneath him. His eyes beaten and nearly swollen shut, he can barely see the sun's dim outline far above him, its bright rays hardly able to touch the earth, eclipsed in darkness. Black vultures swoop in low, lazy circles, stalking, awaiting a victim.

The dull, metallic thud of a heavy hammer rings through the air as two Roman soldiers, one on each side, hammer rusted nails into his flesh. First, the hand of his left outstretched arm feels the excruciating pierce of a six-inch nail. Next, his right hand experiences the pain. His body trembles. His bare, sandaless feet brought together, they too are roughly and cruelly hammered and nailed to the wooden cross.

There now remains only one final act to complete the cruelty. He sees the Roman soldiers that have nailed him to the cross look at each other, hatred gleaming from their contemptuously narrowed eyes. Evil excitement mounts, mingled with anticipation, as the object of their demonic hatred, the carpenter, is about to receive their crowning touch. They grab a nearby circlet of thorns and press it into and upon the top of his head. Blood trickles down onto his swollen, disfigured face. But the soldiers have not yet finished.

In perfect harmony, the Roman soldiers inhale deeply. Their lungs fill then overflow. The overflow fills their cheeks, causing them to balloon outward. Eyes glazed, as one, they exhale their vile curses into the carpenter's face. The hot-aired stench of their putrid breath, mingled with spittle, blast into his face as they verbally mock him. One soldier grabs the left arm of the cross, the other grabs the right arm of the cross, and together they raise the carpenter up off the ground, violently dropping the foot of the cross into a deep hole dug into the dust of Golgotha. A cheer of triumph rises from the gathered crowd. The job is complete. The soldiers agree. It has been a most rewarding day's work.

With a sudden jolt, the carpenter returns to the present. He deeply inhales the night's cool, sweet air. He determinedly pushes all thoughts of the future aside. He takes no more thought in this present for the cost of any of his tomorrows. Long before, in the ageless past, he had already considered the cost of the future.

He has known forever.

He has known that a portion of mankind will believe the only way to stop the carpenter from continuing to create with his hands will be to nail his hands to the arms of a cross. And, to stop his feet from spreading the gospel, they will have to nail his feet also to the foot of the cross. For the present time, mankind has seen him merely as a carpenter. In the future time, all of mankind will eventually see and know that he was, and is, the only begotten son of God.

Jesus the Carpenter, Light of the world, closes the door to his workshop, then walks over to the lamp to blow out its now insufficient, sputtering flame. Night has fallen completely. Today's commissioned work has finished. Tomorrow he will once again enter the workshop to begin another work of commission.

Which one? It really does not matter. Whichever workshop tomorrow's commission holds, whatever the carpenter must fashion, he will prepare it with perfect workmanship.

For he is THE craftsman. THE carpenter.

* * *

Let not your heart be troubled: ye believe in God, believe also in me. In my Father's house are many mansions: if it were not so, I would have told you. I go to prepare a place for you. And if I go and prepare a place for you, I will come again, and receive you unto myself; that where I am, there ye may be also.[4]

---

[4] John 14:1–3

CHAPTER 4

After these things Jesus went over the sea of Galilee, which is the sea of Tiberias.

And a great multitude followed him, because they saw his miracles which he did on them that were diseased.

And Jesus went up into a mountain, and there he sat with his disciples.

And the passover, a feast of the Jew, was nigh.

When Jesus then lifted up his eyes, and saw a great company come unto him, he saith unto Philip, Whence shall we buy bread, that these may eat?

And this he said to prove him: for he himself knew what he would do.

Philip answered him, Two hundred pennyworth of bread is not sufficient for them, that every one of them may take a little.

One of his disciples, Andrew, Simon Peter's brother, saith unto him,

There is a lad here, which hath five barley loaves, and two small fishes: but what are they among so many?

And Jesus said, Make the men sit down. Now there was much grass in the place. So the men sat down, in number about five thousand.

And Jesus took the loaves; and when he had given thanks, he distributed to the disciples, and the disciples to them that were set down; and likewise of the fishes as much as they would.

When they were filled, he said unto his disciples, Gather up the fragments that remain, that nothing be lost.

Therefore they gathered them together, and filled twelve baskets with the fragments of the five barley loaves, which remained over and above unto them that had eaten.

—John 6:1–13

THE SHEPHERD

With so many voices all eagerly speaking at the same time, there was only one thing Jesus could do to resolve the situation. Throwing both his hands up in the air to command their attention, with chagrin he smiled and said, "Hold it down, fellows! Please, just one person at a time."

He was speaking to his twelve chosen disciples. Previously, he had called the twelve disciples together to impart unto them power and authority to cure diseases, and to endue them with power and authority over all devils. Afterward, he had sent them all out, each in traveling groups of two, to heal the sick and to preach the kingdom of God.

After dispersing to surrounding towns to preach the gospel, minister healing to the multitudes of sick, and also to cast out the many devils they encountered everywhere they had traveled, they had all now returned to Capernaum to gather and relate to Jesus of the many deeds they had accomplished, and the teachings they had taught. Although exhausted and hungry, it was, nonetheless, with much passion and enthusiasm they had all begun speaking at the same time, zealous to share with Jesus of their recently assigned accomplishments.

Now, complying with what Jesus had just instructed, one by one they each attempted to relay their individual stories. Due to Passover, a Jewish feast that was nigh, a multitude of noisy groups consisting of both pedestrians and animals busily churned amidst them, at times crowding them out both in bodies and voices, interrupting their narratives. But the disciples remained undaunted. It seemed they were not ever going to run out of words to express the exhilaration, heartache, and challenges they had encountered in their recently assigned responsibilities.

However, Jesus knew even though they were all inspired to continue talking of their spiritual exploits, what they truly needed was to replenish their physical bodies by obtaining food provision and indulging in some much-needed time of leisure for their wearied bodies, for they had only just returned far late into the evening of the previous night. And, it had been awhile that he and his disciples had gathered together privately.

So once again interrupting their speaking, he suggested to them there would be plenty of time later to continue their lively conversations. What was more expedient at the moment was to get to their usual private meeting place near the city of Bethsaida, a journey of about six miles. Located in a remote desert area across the Sea of Galilee, they would all be able to sit down leisurely and partake in fellowship with much more privacy.

To reach the location of their meeting place would require locating and acquiring a ship in the vicinity, for they would need to cross over the Sea of Galilee. The mid-morning was teeming with merchants from which to comply with their desire. Acquiring the necessary sailing vessel, they soon climbed aboard and began the short journey that would take them to the eastern shore of the Sea of Galilee.

As they were departing, having heard Jesus mention the city of Bethsaida, a few of the people standing nearby quickly spread the information as to where Jesus and his disciples were journeying. Because the fame of Jesus and his miracles of healing had become widespread, it did not take long for the news to travel like wildfire among the residents and travelers of the area. Soon there was a great multitude of people, even those from the small towns round about, that followed after Jesus, on foot, along the shorelines north and east, for there were many that were diseased and in need of healing.

Upon arriving at the eastern shore of the Sea of Galilee, near Bethsaida, the ship dropped anchor, and Jesus and his disciples departed from aboard the ship. Resuming their journey, with Jesus in the lead, they trailed after him to begin the foot passage required to reach their final destination.

More often than not, taking a trek such as they were now undertaking was a potentially dangerous journey. All sorts of wild beasts such as bears and lions roamed the land, along with various species of poisonous vipers. But Jesus had led them through this area on many other occasions and by this time, after three years of being under his discipleship, they all well knew the precautions they needed to heed for the safest way of passage.

Once they had reached the narrow expanse of the waterless and dismal desert, in the shimmering distance they could see their destination, the mountain of which Jesus was so fond, where he frequently took his disciples to teach them privately. Away from the crowded and noisy communities dotting the areas that surrounded the still waters of Galilee, it was always a quiet haven of temporary retreat and solitude. In the course of his ministry, it had also become a favorite place of private refuge for Jesus when he had desired to be alone in prayer with his heavenly Father.

Continuing on, still following Jesus, the disciples proceeded across the sunburned desert ground, their sandaled feet kicking up little clouds of dusty air until they reached the foot of the mountain. Ascending the short distance near to the top, the disciples seated themselves gratefully down upon the luxuriant green grass that covered the mountain and its base. Lounging upon the coolness of the grass was refreshing, and within moments, the disciples, revived, began to swap stories amongst themselves of their previous encounters, still impassioned over their recent adventures.

Taking advantage of the opportunity, Jesus sat himself down near his disciples. Closing his eyes briefly, in prayer, he took the moment to commune with his heavenly Father. He so loved the Father and continually yearned for the stillness to be with Him and hear His voice.

Moments later, Jesus opened and raised his eyes. As he did so, he beheld a great company of men, women, and children numbering around five-thousand, silently streaming across the scorched desert land, approaching the mountain where he and his disciples now sat upon its summit. His heart became instantly overwhelmed with compassion toward them for he saw they were as sheep without a shepherd. Discerning they were desperately in need of care, Jesus arose, eager to enfold and personally shepherd this great flock of people.

Aware that Jesus had suddenly jumped-up, his disciples straightway ceased their animated discussions. Turning their heads in the direction in which Jesus was peering, they too beheld the great flock of people approaching the mountain. As they quietly observed, Jesus stretched out his arms toward the great multitude with a welcoming gesture. The great mass gathered, filling the mountain and its base with a sea of humanity, all yearning and gazing upward with need and hope.

As any devoted and loving shepherd would do for any untended flock, Jesus began attending, without delay, to all their need. Discerning the multitude was starving from spiritual hunger, as the next few hours passed, he first taught them many things of the kingdom of God, feeding them the life-giving words. Once he had accomplished that, he then set about to minister healing to those that needed relief from their many sicknesses. Perceiving their every need and want, he would not allow them to lack for anything. He was fulfilling, in part, that which he had longed to come to earth to do, spoken and foretold of him in the Holy Scriptures.

The Lord is my shepherd; I shall not want...

Ministering to so many, the daytime soon waned. As the evening drew nigh, the disciples knew the great company of people had to be physically hungry, for no one, including their own selves, had eaten of any food the entire day. With hunger gnawing at their stomachs, the disciples discussed the matter among their own selves and quickly decided they should speak to Jesus about the matter.

While the other disciples stood clustered as a group close by, acting as a spokesman for the disciples, Philip walked over to where Jesus was standing amongst the crowd. Pulling Jesus aside, speaking as quietly as possible, Philip presented the problem, as he and the disciples viewed it, to Jesus. He pointed out to Jesus that it was getting very late, and no one had yet eaten anything the entire day.

Jesus answered Philip by simply asking, "And where are we to buy food so everyone can eat?"

Jesus, knowing what he himself had in mind and was preparing to do, only asked the question of Philip in order to test him. Jesus was attempting to stretch Philip's newly obtained faith in administering miracles that, only hours ago, Philip had been speaking of so passionately and tirelessly.

Philip, however, was not at that moment able to see beyond what his natural eyes were observing. Philip remarked that even if they used all the money they had in their treasury, two-hundred pennyworth, to purchase only bread it would not be enough to feed every person even a small morsel. He also reminded Jesus that besides not having enough money, they just happened to be out in the middle of the desert and there was not a place nearby to purchase any food even if they wanted!

In his developing anxiety, he had even suggested to Jesus that perhaps they should send the multitude of people away to travel into the surrounding villages, while there was yet still daylight, so that they might purchase something for themselves to eat. After all, besides men, there were women and children in consideration.

Jesus, still seeking to flame a spark of faith within any of his disciples, turned and asked of the remaining eleven, "Are you certain there is nothing here to eat?"

A few of the disciples looked at each other quizzically, and a couple even shrugged their shoulders at one another, as if to say, "*I don't know what he's talking about...do you?*"

However, one of the twelve, Simon Peter's brother, Andrew, looking once again upon the crowd, saw something that he had not taken notice of previously. A young boy with a basket of five barley loaves of bread, along with two small fishes, was standing nearby. Pointing out the lad, he said to Jesus, "Well, there *is* this one little boy here with his basket of five barley loaves of bread and two fishes. But that would not even begin to feed the multitude that is gathered here!"

Jesus, observing that once again his disciples were sorely lacking in faith, did not immediately reply. He moved his gaze to peer beyond the great multitude gathered before him, seeing behind the small stretch of arid desert that the sun was beginning to sink toward the horizon. The brilliance of the setting sun's glorious light was magnifying and reflecting in the distant, still waters of the Sea of Galilee.

Glancing once again upon the people standing before him upon the emerald green grass, Jesus, the Shepherd, simply gave a directive to his disciples. He stated, "Make all the men sit down."

He maketh me to lie down in green pastures: he leadeth me beside the still waters...

His disciples busily and methodically began to obey his directive, making the men sit down in groups of fifty upon the lush, green grass. When all had settled, speaking to his disciples, Jesus requested them to bring to him the little boy's basket of food. Wondering what Jesus was going to do next, the disciples curiously obeyed his instructions.

Taking into his hands the basket containing the five barley loaves and two fishes, Jesus paused for a moment, reflecting silently within his heart before speaking. "Father, I have taken these lost sheep you sent to me and have satisfied their soul's hunger. I have given unto them your life-giving words to show them the path of your righteousness."

He restoreth my soul: he leadeth me in the paths of righteousness for his name's sake...

"Most have encountered many dark times in life and today braved the perilous journey to follow and find me, searching for hope and comfort. As they now stand in this desert valley before me restored in soul and comforted, they no longer have reason to fear the evils of life."

Yea, though I walk through the valley of the shadow of death, I will fear no evil: for thou art with me: thy rod and thy staff they comfort me...

"Now, Father, anoint me to perform another miracle. That as a Good Shepherd, I may also provide for my sheep's physical hunger."

Looking upward to heaven, smiling knowingly at his heavenly Father, Jesus audibly blessed the Father, giving thanks for the banquet table which was about to be prepared. Breaking apart the five loaves of bread and the two fishes, Jesus began to disburse the food to his disciples, instructing them to distribute the food to the multitude.

And so it was that the bread and fishes did multiply, and they did all eat until filled. Everyone, including his disciples, feasted in pleasure and safety as Jesus, their Shepherd, kept watch over them.

Wanting nothing wasted, Jesus asked his disciples to gather up the food that remained. The disciples went among the multitude to gather the fragments together. And lo and behold! It took twelve baskets to hold all that remained, filled to the brims, with the leftover bread and fish.

Thou preparest a table before me in the presence of mine enemies: thou anointest my head with oil; my cup runneth over...

As the sun began slipping below the horizon and darkness was beginning to fall, Jesus watched as the great company of people made ready to depart. They had come to him filled with fear and despair. They were leaving filled with faith and assurance.

As their Shepherd, he had taught the flock of his Father's goodness and mercy, assuring all of the Father's everlasting love for them. Forever they would remain his flock, and forever he would remain their Shepherd. He had taught them he would soon lay down his life for them and return to the Father, but they were not to fear his departure. For one day, he would come back for them, and they would live with him and the Father forever.

Surely goodness and mercy shall follow me all the days of my life: and I will dwell in the house of the Lord forever.[5]

* * *

Then said Jesus unto them again, Verily, verily, I say unto you, I am the door of the sheep. All that ever came before me are thieves and robbers: but the sheep did not hear them. I am the door: by me if any man enter in, he shall be saved, and shall go in and out, and find pasture. The thief cometh not, but for to steal, and to kill, and to destroy: I am come that they might have life, and that they might have it more abundantly. I am the good shepherd: the good shepherd giveth his life for the sheep.[6]

---

[5] Psalms 23:1–6
[6] John 10:7–11

CHAPTER 5

And out of the ground the Lord God formed every beast of the field, and every fowl of the air; and brought them unto Adam to see what he would call them: and whatsoever Adam called every living creature, that was the name thereof;

And Adam gave names to all cattle, and to the fowl of the air, and to every beast of the field; but for Adam there was not found an help meet for him.

And the Lord God caused a deep sleep to fall upon Adam, and he slept: and he took one of his ribs, and closed up the flesh instead thereof;

And the rib, which the Lord God had taken from man, made he a woman, and brought her unto the man.

And Adam said, This is now bone of my bones, and flesh of my flesh: she shall be called Woman, because she was taken out of Man.

Therefore shall a man leave his father and his mother, and shall cleave unto his wife: and they shall be one flesh.

And they were both naked, the man and his wife, and were not ashamed.

—Genesis 2:19–25

THE BRIDE

Strolling leisurely on his way to the Tree of Life, Adam stopped to kick his toe into the moist, dark earth of the garden's soil, a tuft of the soil landing directly in his path. He stooped over to pick up the clump of earth in his hand, and as he did, he noticed the soil felt warm and soft to the touch. He could not resist bringing the clump of earth to his nostrils to breathe in its fresh, clean smell. How he loved his beautiful garden, this paradise and all it contained.

The garden paradise, just eastward in Eden, was Adam's home. The Father had previously created and planted it just for him. When the Father first brought Adam into the garden, the Father had proudly announced to him everything within the garden now belonged exclusively to Adam. With a flourish of his arm, the Father had invited Adam to inspect and explore his new home. The Father had expressed to him he was confident Adam would enjoy all he would find; for the Father had made certain everything the garden contained was very pleasant and very fruitful.

Adam had found the garden to be everything the Father had said it would be. Every herb bearing seed, every fruit-bearing tree was, indeed, lush and bountiful. The garden was pleasantly fragrant with the teeming mixed aromas of dill, cumin, coriander, sesame, and mint. Other aromatic herbs included anise, myrtle, camphor, hyssop, and saffron. In one section, the garden abounded with cucumbers, melons, leeks, onions, and garlic. In another, along hilly knolls, overflowing grapevines twined their trails, heavily laden with huge clusters of grapes. In yet another dense portion of the garden, Adam had also found beans and lentils growing.

Overhead, treetops provided a leafy canopy for Adam's home, the canopy branches encumbered with a diverse mixture of ripened fruits. Figs, avocados, olives, nuts, apples, apricots, oranges, and dates dripped in profusion, affording Adam with the tastiest of meals any time he hungered. Every tree pleasant to the sight and good for sustenance existed within the garden paradise. In the midst of the profuse garden, Adam had also discovered the location of a single tree of knowledge of good and evil, and the solitary tree of life.

As he continued his walk along the banks of the river that watered the garden as it flowed outward of Eden, Adam noticed a dazzling new array of flowers had burst forth in bloom. White lotus blossoms and lilies lazily floated upon the river's water surface, while blue-purplish hyacinths, along with deep yellow narcissus and pale pink tulips, now dotted the river's shoreline. Farther in from the river's banks, the aroma from various colored rose bushes filled the garden's cool evening air with their intoxicating fragrance, causing Adam to inhale their perfumed scent with delight.

This garden was truly a paradise. The Father had explained to Adam one evening during their nightly ritual of walking and talking together in the cool of the evening, that Adam was to have absolute dominion over the garden. He was to keep it cultivated and also guard and protect it from all intruders. In return for his labor, Adam would eat, nourished with all the garden contained. In this way, he would receive sustenance for all eternity, lacking nothing. The Father also informed him that of every tree within the garden he could partake of and eat freely.

With one exception.

Adam was *not* to eat of the tree of the knowledge of good and evil. The Father was very vehement in voice as he had commanded Adam never to eat of it; for in the day he should partake of it, Adam would surely die a spiritual death. In addition, if Adam were to die spiritually, eventually, he would also suffer a physical death. As further warning, the Father also gravely warned Adam if he chose to disobey this instruction, not only would he lose the promise of eternal life, the Father would also expel Adam from the garden.

Adam understood. He knew the Father's only intention and purpose was to provide, delight, and cover him with nothing less than loving-kindness and goodness.

With much enjoyment, the Father had also brought unto Adam every beast of the field, and every fowl of the air, respectfully requesting of Adam what to name each creature. Whatsoever name Adam had advised, the Father had replied, "So be it!" They had had such a great time together as they accomplished the task. There were times when they had even resounded in hilarious, raucous laughter as some of the more comically shaped and fashioned living creatures came forth to receive a name.

As he thought back to the day when he and the Father had completed that task, Adam now realized a feeling of melancholy had been with him ever since. This wistfulness began to occur as the Father had brought forth the living creatures for Adam to name. Adam had noticed the Father had created each one of the creatures a male and a female. When Adam had questioned the Father as to why he had created all the creatures in such a manner, the Father told Adam he had done so simply to bless them. The creatures would find companionship in a counterpoint of their own kind. In return, they would be fruitful and multiply, and able to replenish the earth.

Adam fondly noted, as the Father had continued to explain many other things to him, the Father had a favorite expression of explanation. "I just saw that it was good to do so."

Adam trusted the Father's reasoning and knew if the Father saw that it was good, then surely it must be rightly so. However, Adam had not been able to help but notice that for *him* there was no created female companion. This wistfulness within Adam was so troubling; he decided to bring the matter to the Father's attention this night in their walk together in the cool of the evening. Adam knew the Father would be able to explain the thoughts and feelings he was experiencing because he knew the Father knew all things. His Father was so knowledgeable; he always knew just the right thing to say and do at all times.

Arriving at the tree of life in the midst of the garden, Adam contentedly sat down upon the ground beneath. With his naked back pressed against the tree's rough bark, Adam wanted to quietly rest underneath its luxuriant boughs for just a moment. It was such a pleasant spot. The evening's soft breeze gently touched and kissed his handsome face as he sat with eyes closed, awaiting the arrival of the Father. This was the calm and peaceful part of the day and though the sun was just beginning to slip below the horizon, its warmth still radiated from the earth upon which Adam now sat.

Adam's thoughts began to wander. He was feeling so very sleepy. The yearning within his soul was still present, yet he had an odd sense it would soon depart from him. As lethargy continued to spill over him, although knowing the Father was due to arrive at any moment, he felt himself limply tumble toward sleep. Why, he could even hear the Father's voice now in the distance and he so wanted to speak with him. But he just could not seem to pull himself up out of the sleepiness that was now heavily upon him. As he drifted and descended into a deeper sleep, he could hear the Father, as if talking to himself, saying, "It is not good that Adam should be alone; I will make a companion suitable for him."

And while Adam reposed in a deep sleep the Father had placed upon him, the Father set about to remedy the source of Adam's recent melancholic disquietude. He opened up the flesh of Adam's side, just below his arm. Blood poured forth from Adam's wounded side as the Father removed a single rib. To stanch the blood that flowed from the wound, with just a touch of his finger, he cauterized the flesh of Adam's side. After doing so, from the bone of Adam's rib, the Father continued his task at hand, skillfully forming a female companion for Adam. A bride.

The Father had carefully chosen the site from which he had selected to fashion Adam's bride. The Father did not take her from Adam's head to be domineered by him. Nor did he take her from Adam's feet to be trampled by him. Instead, the Father took her from Adam's side to be equal with him, from under his arm to be protected by him. And from near his heart to be loved by him.

Having lovingly completed his work, he now removed the deep sleep from Adam he had caused. Smiling to himself, the Father eagerly waited for Adam to regain consciousness. He could hardly contain his anticipation for Adam's soon-to-be discovery.

Moments later, Adam's eyes fluttered open and instantly beheld the Father's gift. There stood before him the most beautiful creature his eyes had ever encountered. She was like him, yet different. Why, she was a female, after his own kind! A womb-man. A companion and helper.

Jumping to his feet, Adam felt a twinge from his side, and immediately he discerned she was from out of him, fashioned from his own body. And now here she stood, placed before him by the Father.

The Father, with a twinkle in his eyes, now asked, "Well, Adam, what's your opinion? What should she be called?"

With jubilation, Adam replied, "Because she is of my body, and of my flesh, and of my bones, she shall be called Woman. Together, my bride and I shall be one flesh."

Smiling, the father blessed Adam and his bride, saying to them, "Be fruitful my children, and multiply. Go, replenish the earth, and subdue it."

And the Father saw everything he had made, and behold, it was now *very* good.

* * *

On Calvary's barren hill, his naked back pressed against the rough bark of a tree trunk hewn and crudely fashioned into a cross, in the cool of the evening, the lifeless body of Jesus, the last Adam, hung limply. The evening's soft breeze gently touched and kissed his now disfigured face.

The angry crowd had long before dispersed. Earlier, the Jewish people among the witnessing crowds had left to go inform Pilate that the body of Jesus, along with the two others crucified with him, should not remain hanging upon the crosses until the next day. It would be unlawful to do so since the next day would be their holy Sabbath day.

They besought Pilate to send his soldiers to break the legs of those hanging on the crosses, expediting their deaths. The soldiers could then remove the bodies expediently before the Jewish Sabbath.

Pilate had sent his soldiers to comply with their wishes. The soldiers stood now before the first criminal crucified and proceeded to break his legs to hasten his death. This they also did to the second criminal. But when his soldiers came to Jesus, they observed that he was already dead and there was no need to break his legs.

Nevertheless, one of the soldiers took the spear he was carrying and thrust it into Jesus and pierced his side, just under his arm, next to a rib, causing the blood and water within the heart of Jesus to pour forth.

Unknowingly to the soldier, his act fulfilled that which the scriptures foretold. For as Jesus Christ loved the church and gave his life for it, and as his blood and water poured forth from within him, his bride was formed and fashioned by the Father. From Jesus' pierced side, the church was born, a beautiful and glorious bride, not having spot or wrinkle, or any such thing. She was holy and without blemish.

For the Father had carefully chosen the site to take from and fashion the last Adam's bride. She was not formed from Christ's head to be domineered by him, nor did he take her from Christ's feet to be trampled by him. Instead, the Father took her from Christ's side to be equal with him, from under his arm to be protected by him. And from near his heart to be loved by him.

And the Father saw everything he had made, and behold, it was now *very* good.

* * *

Husbands, love your wives, even as Christ also loved the church, and gave himself for it; that he might sanctify and cleanse it with the washing of water by the word, that he might present it to himself a glorious church, not having spot, or wrinkle, or any such thing; but that it should be holy and without blemish.[7]

---

[7] Ephesians 5:25–27

CHAPTER 6

Then Jesus six days before the passover came to Bethany, where Lazarus was which had been dead, whom he raised from the dead.

There they made him a supper; and Martha served: but Lazarus was one of them that sat at the table with him.

Then took Mary a pound of ointment of spikenard, very costly, and anointed the feet of Jesus, and wiped his feet with her hair: and the house was filled with the odour of the ointment.

Then saith one of his disciples, Judas Iscariot, Simon's son, which should betray him,

Why was not this ointment sold for three hundred pence, and given to the poor?

This he said, not that he cared for the poor; but because he was a thief, and had the bag, and bare what was put therein.

Then said Jesus, Let her alone: against the day of my burying hath she kept this.

For the poor always ye have with you; but me ye have not always.

—John 12:1–8

THE MEMORIAL

Within the well-appointed dwelling located in the small town of Bethany, there was much cheerful and lively conversation amidst the clanking and clattering of earthenware pots and jars as Martha and Mary busily prepared for the impending evening's supper. The supper was to be a celebration among those who would be the gathered guests.

Martha had taken it upon herself to be in charge of orchestrating everything needed to provide the utmost in hospitality for all who would be present. She found no greater joy than in being a hostess, or in the cooking and serving of a meal. Martha was known far and wide for these talents she possessed, and in being able to prepare a delicious and tasty feast from just the most ordinary of food staples.

Mary could not help but smile to herself as she glanced at her elder sister, observing the look of pure joy now shining upon Martha's countenance. Martha, up to her stout elbows in barley flour, was obviously ecstatic.

Mary knew Martha had given great thought to this particular evening's meal. This supper was to be a celebrated occasion, for they had also invited a very beloved friend, Jesus, to be the guest of honor. He would also be bringing along several of his disciples to join the celebration.

Jesus, who greatly loved Martha, Mary, and their brother, Lazarus, had visited and dined with them privately many times past in their home, for they were all the closest of friends. However, this occasion was to be especially festive because it would be their first time visiting with Jesus since the day he had miraculously resurrected Lazarus from the tomb.

Oh, that glorious and triumphant day had been one Mary and Martha would never forget. For on that day they had witnessed their only brother, Lazarus, walk forth from the tomb after buried and encased in death for four days! The entire town of Bethany still could not refrain from talking about that day's astonishing miracle.

Therefore, when they had since received news Jesus and his disciples were returning from Ephraim to Bethany in order to participate in the Feast of Passover and the Feast of Unleavened Bread, it had been the perfect opportunity for Lazarus and his sisters to offer invitation for Jesus to visit and dine with them once more. As soon as Jesus had sent word that he would gladly accept their invitation, Martha began to make certain to closely attend to every detail.

Martha, Mary, and Lazarus had each concurred this supper was to be the very best they could proffer. After all, the guest of honor was Jesus! Martha had immediately occupied herself with organizing a list of everything she would need to prepare the meal. For the last week, Mary and Lazarus had run to and fro; gathering and purchasing the seemingly endless items Martha had so painstakingly inventoried and listed.

Martha procured a choice, tender lamb. Salted fish, locust beans, lentils, eggs, olive oil, flours of barley and wheat, wine, honey, fresh and dried figs, grapes, dates, raisins, melons, almonds, pomegranates, and Martha pistachios, all purchased throughout the week, now lay in colorful profusion inside coarsely-plaited reed baskets scattered throughout the room. Gallons of water, fetched from the local well by Martha earlier that morning, stood in large earthenware pitchers placed underneath the table on the spotlessly clean fieldstone floor.

Always a fastidious housekeeper, Martha had earlier insisted all things portable, in every room of the house, taken outside so she could thoroughly sweep and wash the stone floors. Even the thick walls and many niches, used for storing food and utensils, had not escaped scrubbing until the limestone dully gleamed. Martha and Mary removed from the floors all the hand-woven rugs, hanging them outside, and had beaten them with a broom of straw so as to disengage any particle of hidden dirt that might have lurked within.

In the glazed lamps placed on projections protruding from the plastered walls, all flaxen wicks trimmed, the lamp bowls now stood fully filled and fueled with olive oil. Kindling sticks and wood from the white broom plant lay gathered and arranged near the recessed fireplace in order to make certain there would be plenty of fuel for all the cooking required. The ample supply of fuel would also make provision for warmth later in the evening when the air would become cold and damp.

They carefully considered everything possible in providing total hospitality for all invited guests.

The juicy, perfectly roasted choice lamb now occupied the central place of honor upon the heavy-planked kitchen table. The only task left remaining to complete was the baking of the barley bread and Martha had it well in hand, now in the process of mixing barley flour with water to make the bread dough. Mary, although having assisted with the cleaning and shopping, knew she would not be of much use to Martha from this point on. Martha, it seemed, had inherited all of the talent and skills in the family for cooking.

Involuntarily, Mary sighed. Her lack of ability in this area had caused problems between her and Martha on many past occasions. Martha had even once implied it was just due to laziness that Mary was not interested in developing an enthusiasm for preparing and serving meals. Martha just could not seem to understand why it was that Mary did not want to be cooking at every given opportunity.

It was not that Mary was lazy. Although frail and delicate in stature, she had always performed more than her share of the necessary housework and chores. But lately, it seemed she was increasingly finding herself drawn to solitary prayer and meditating upon all the words of teaching Jesus had shared with her during their many previous visits.

Since the day she had first met Jesus, she simply had not been the same woman. A wonderful transformation had taken place within her heart and spirit. But this inward hunger and thirst for being more and more in prayer that she was now experiencing was not something she could easily explain to Martha. Or to anyone else, for that matter. Even today, in the midst of all preparations for the evening's supper, the past several hours she once again had been longing in her spirit to be alone in prayer.

The desire in her spirit was not something she could ignore any longer. Glancing at Martha again, she wondered if she should mention anything about it to Martha.

Thoroughly engrossed in her task, Martha hummed softly as she deftly continued kneading the bread dough. Not wanting to cause Martha to become distraught, Mary decided she would refrain from speaking to her about the matter. Instead, she decided on quietly attempting to slip out of the room, unnoticed. She would do so in order to go to the privacy of her own room, planning to pray for just a little while, then return and help Martha as best she could.

Treading softly, Mary successfully escaped to her room located at the opposite end of their dwelling, carefully closing the door while listening intently for any sign Martha may have noticed her departure. Mary was fairly confident her exit from the kitchen had gone unnoticed, but she wanted to be certain.

All remained quiet throughout the house.

Now fully assured of her privacy, with worshipful longing compelling her to her knees, she knelt and began her prayer in the peaceful solitude of seclusion. Within moments, her heart and spirit began to soar heavenward and soon she became unaware of her earthly surroundings. Her mind began to fill with the many things of which Jesus had spoken in the past as she had sat, always at his feet, learning all she could, drinking in his every word. Curiously, as if searching for something she had overlooked, it now seemed her heart was becoming even more restless.

Praying for understanding of that for which her heart was searching, Mary continued to reflect on the words and teachings of her beloved Jesus. Her mind swirling with so many thoughts, she did not notice as the remaining day waned. The shadows in her small room grew longer and longer.

Outside, on the narrow street adjacent to her room, a shepherd and his flock were traveling through town, en route to Jerusalem two miles farther. From the tiny, open window across her room floated the sounds of a tinkling bell and the bleating of lambs. The sounds pierced and interrupted her reveries, bringing to her remembrance the Jewish Passover Festival currently in observance.

Due to observance of the seven-day Jewish Passover Festival, over a quarter million male lambs were in Jerusalem, shepherded and sold for the Feast of the Passover. On the first day of the festival, the tenth day of the month, every Jewish household would purchase a male lamb without blemish. On the fourteenth day of the month, each household would then take their purchased lamb to the Temple, and at three o'clock that evening the temple priests would start the slaying of the lambs. The temple priests were then to begin to offer the blood of each slain lamb as a sacrifice upon the altar in the Temple.

As the temple priests accomplished the blood sacrifices, they then hung the carcasses of the slain lambs. Each family would then quickly take the lamb carcass back to their home. The same evening, they were to roast their lamb upon a spit of pomegranate wood, one male lamb for each household, and consummately eat of it, thus fulfilling the Lord's Passover Feast requirements and traditions of celebration and remembrance.

Each Jewish family performed this ritual as a memorial unto the Lord. It was an established celebration of remembrance for a past event, while in their sojourn in Egypt, in which the Lord had delivered them from their bondage of slavery. It was also a commemorate celebration for the Jewish families because the event had ultimately led to their departure from Egypt.

The event had occurred when, in order to at last free them from the Egyptians, the Lord sent an angel of death to pass through Egypt and smite the firstborn, both man and beast. On that past occasion, the Lord made only one exception in the smiting of all firstborn. With instructions he gave solely to the children of Israel, the Lord directed each household of the Israelites to kill a spotless male lamb that had no blemish and then to apply the blood of that slain lamb to the upper doorpost and two side posts of their doorways on the night the angel of death appeared. Upon their doing so, the Lord would command the death angel to ignore the homes upon which was found the blood.

The Israelites had complied, and death did not strike the households with the blood of a spotless male lamb applied to the upper doorpost and two side posts of the doorway. The angel of death had "passed over" the homes of these families, sparing the firstborn of all the Israelites, in adherence to the Lord's instruction of exception. It was for this exception the Passover Feast had been instituted by the Lord and celebrated annually by the Jewish people ever since.

As Mary remembered, pondering the purpose of the now occurring Passover Festival, in the distance, she could hear the diminishing sound of the passing shepherd herding his bleating flock of lambs. Something quickened in her heart. Unexpectedly, a recollection of what one of the disciples had once told her came to her mind. He had heard John, the Baptist, speak it when he first saw Jesus coming unto him. He had said, "Behold the Lamb of God, which taketh away the sin of the world."[8]

Suddenly, with crystal clarity, Mary knew and understood the enormity of that which John, the Baptist, had spoken. She now comprehended the supreme sacrifice Jesus had come to earth to offer as the spotless Lamb of God. And within her spirit, she knew the time to offer himself as the ultimate sacrifice was now very near.

With her heart pounding, her eyes flew open. A fading beam of sunlight softly directed her sight to light upon her most prized possession. It stood tucked away in a corner, an alabastra vessel that contained a pound of very costly, perfumed ointment. With an aching love, Mary knew now what she must do.

Running across the shadowed room, Mary reached down to pick up the ivory-colored vessel containing the ointment. As she did, she also became aware of many voices coming from the other end of their dwelling. One of the voices was that of Jesus. The entire afternoon had passed by without her even realizing it! However, the time that had passed by was now of small consequence. Her heart focused on the only thing that truly mattered to her.

---

[8]   John 1:29

Jesus.

Crossing the room again, tightly clutching the container of precious ointment, Mary rushed out of her room and made her way to the room where all the guests had already gathered. Upon entering the room, Mary vaguely noticed the evening meal was already in progress, with Martha busily serving all those in attendance. But Mary had eyes only for Jesus who now directly faced her, reclining at the table. Calmly, Jesus raised his eyes and met her unwavering gaze.

And he perceived that she knew.

Stepping to where Jesus reclined, Mary knelt humbly before him, her eyes never leaving his as she continued to look knowingly into his face. The soft lamplight etched the streaming tears of love and understanding that now glistened upon her upturned face. In that one small moment, their eyes said everything words could not express.

The flask of ointment still held tightly in her right hand, Mary dropped her gaze to remove the seal from the vessel's long, slender top. Carefully placing the alabastra vessel down onto the stone floor, she reached up with both hands to loosen her long dark hair from atop her head, permitting it to cascade freely down the length of her back. Mary then took the now opened alabastra flask, worth nearly a year's wages, and began pouring from it the costly perfumed ointment. She poured out the vessel's entire contents, anointing the feet of Jesus.

Still kneeling, Mary bent forward, causing her long luxuriant tresses to tumble onto his feet. Reverently, she began lovingly to wipe his anointed feet with her hair. She sacrificed and poured forth the costliest of that which she had to offer. Knowing soon he too would sacrifice and pour forth the costliest of that which *he* had to offer, his very life's blood, this she did as a memorial unto him.

The surplus remaining of the poured fragrant ointment dripped downward from the feet of Jesus onto the floor, forming an aromatic puddle, seeping into the pores of the stones where the fragrance would remain even years afterward. The aroma of the perfumed ointment filled the air, permeating the nostrils of those who were present, overwhelming all.

For a moment, no one spoke a word. The only sound heard in that moment was the sound of Mary's weeping. And as all others sat silently, the entire house became filled with the sweet-smelling fragrance of the ointment of her sacrifice.

* * *

About the sixth hour, which for the Jewish was at noon, on the fourteenth day of Nisan during the Jewish Passover, the sun darkened, and gross darkness covered the entire earth. It remained until the ninth hour. At the ninth hour, three o'clock in the evening, a thunderous yet pitiful collective bleating of lamb's voices became heard as the Jewish priests began the start of the slaying of nearly a quarter of a million lambs within the Temple in Jerusalem, in preparation for the Passover Feast.

At the same exact time, one lone lamb's voice stood out from the rest. It too was thunderous. However, instead of pitiful, it was triumphant. It came not from the Temple in Jerusalem, but from Golgotha's lonely hill just outside of Jerusalem. Hanging crucified upon a cross, with his last dying breath, the Lamb's voice cried out, "It is finished!"

Sacrificing and pouring forth that which was the costliest he had to offer, his very life's blood, this he did as a memorial unto all generations. Some standing near the foot of the cross became bewildered by the aroma of a perfumed ointment that began to fill the air permeating their nostrils, overwhelming all who were present.

As Jesus bowed his head and life departed from him, for a moment, no one spoke a word. The only sound heard in that moment was the sound of weeping from the few who had loved him. And as all who had been witnesses remained and stood silently, a gentle breeze began to blow. Catching the aromatic scent of the perfumed ointment, it caused the aroma to continue to rise and waft upward far into the heavens above. And so it was that the entire house of God became filled with the sweet-smelling fragrance of the sacrifice.

* * *

Be ye therefore followers of God, as dear children; And walk in love, as Christ also hath loved us, and hath given himself for us an offering and a sacrifice to God for a sweetsmelling savour.[9]

---

[9] Ephesians 5:1–2

CHAPTER 7

And this shall be a statute for ever unto you: that in the seventh month, on the tenth day of the month, ye shall afflict your souls, and do no work at all, whether it be one of your own country, or a stranger that sojourned among you:

For on that day shall the priest make an atonement for you, to cleanse you, that ye may be clean from all your sins before the Lord.

It shall be a Sabbath of rest unto you, and ye shall afflict your souls, by a statute for ever.

And the priest, whom he shall anoint, and whom he shall consecrate to minister in the priest's office in his father's stead, shall make the atonement, and shall put on the linen clothes, even the holy garments:

And he shall make an atonement for the holy sanctuary, and he shall make an atonement for the tabernacle of the congregation, and for the altar, and he shall make an atonement for the priests, and for all the people of the congregation.

And this shall be an everlasting statute unto you, to make atonement for the children of Israel for all their sins once a year. And he did as the Lord commanded Moses.

—Leviticus 16:29–34

THE BLOOD

The blistering hot, arid desert wind howled as it furiously spit stinging sand at anything in its pathway. However, all was quiet within the innermost tent of the Tabernacle which stood pitched in its path on the Egyptian desert of Mount Sinai. Located within the Tabernacle's courtyard, the Tabernacle's innermost tent of fine twined linen lay covered with curtains of black goat hair and an over-laying covering of rams' skins dyed red. Topped-off with an additional layer of badger skins, it offered an elaborate protection and quiet shelter from all harshness of the wild desert wilderness.

Pitched round-about the outer perimeter of the Tabernacle courtyard was the great encampment of the families of the twelve tribes of Israel, over six million people, according to the order of their tribes: to the west the tribes of Benjamin, Ephraim, and Manasseh; to the north the tribes of Asher, Dan, and Naphtali; to the east the tribes of Zebulon, Judah, and Issachar; and to the south the tribes of Simeon, Reuben, and Gad.

On this tenth day of the seventh month of the Hebrew calendar, October, there was no work performed by any of the great encampment of people. Each family remained within their own tent, fasting and afflicting their souls. For on this day only, no one worked or entered any court of the Tabernacle until the High Priest performed the sacrifices and rituals necessary for atonement.

This special Sabbath day of rest and fasting, newly instituted by the Lord, was to henceforth occur on this date every year following. The Lord had newly established it in order to provide collectively and annually, a way of means of reconciliation for all their sins, including the sins of both High Priest and the people of the congregation. The Lord declared from this day hence that forever it was to be known as the great Day of Atonement.

This first day of his officiating the duties for the great Day of Atonement, having already exercised the ordinary, daily ritual of the office of High Priest, Aaron had just begun to commence the newly appropriated ceremonies. Standing within the inner courtyard of the Tabernacle, strictly adhering to the Lord's detailed instructions, he had removed from his body the ornate garments of High Priest and washed at the brass laver in the Tabernacle's courtyard. He was now preparing to dress in the stipulated garments worn only while performing the sacrifices and duties necessary for the great Day of Atonement. Once he had made the required atonement sacrifices, he would then be able to enter into the most holy place beyond the veil of separation, the Holy of Holies, where the Ark of the Covenant stood. It was there the Lord would appear to Aaron, in a cloud of glory upon the ark's beaten-gold mercy seat and officially accept the atonement sacrifices.

On every other occasion in which he officiated and ministered as the High Priest, the usual attire of his office consisted of various articles of much splendor: a fine twined linen ephod interlaced with threads of blue, purple, scarlet, and beaten threads of gold; an ephod girdle, or belt, fashioned of the same materials as the ephod; a breastplate, also made of the same materials as the ephod, but additionally adorned by settings of precious stones, four rows of three, with each stone engraved according to the twelve tribes of Israel; a robe of woven work, blue in color, all of one piece, its flowing skirt's hem embellished round-about with pomegranates of three colors intertwined of blue, purple, and scarlet, with each pomegranate alternated by a bell of pure gold; an embroidered coat, or tunic, the innermost garment, woven of pure white fine linen; and a mitre, or crowning headdress, of fine white wound linen banded on the forefront with an engraved plate of pure gold.

However, on this great Day of Atonement, the Lord had given Aaron's brother, Moses, a new directive concerning the garments the

High Priest was to wear. When performing the Day of Atonement sacrifices, duties and requirements, Aaron was not to array himself in the robes of glory, beauty, and dignity ordinarily representative of the office of High Priest. Instead, Aaron was to go before the Lord in simplicity and humility. Therefore, the holy garments worn would consist simply of a coat without seam, a belt, breeches, and a mitre; all made of pure white linen only.

As Aaron now slowly and carefully unfolded the pure white priestly linen garments, his hands visibly trembled. For just two days earlier, on their very first day of anointing and consecration to the office of priest, two of his sons, Nadab and Abihu, had died while attempting to minister as priests before the hallowed presence of the Lord.

The calamity had befallen them in the course of performing their priestly duties within the Tabernacle. As they sought to light the incense they had placed within the golden censers, self-exalted and in a state of drunkenness, Nadab and Abihu had attempted to offer a strange fire, of their own making, to light the incense. Contrary to the specific instructions of conduct the Lord had previously given them, they had used a fire not taken from off the brazen altar. In doing so, they had blatantly violated the holy services of their sacred office.

So hot was the Lord's displeasure at their conduct, a burning fire had blazed from out of the Lord's presence, devouring them. Both had died, instantly, as they stood in the blast of the Lord's holy wrath.

Two of Aaron's first cousins, Mishael and Elzaphan, commanded by Aaron's brother, Moses, approached the Tabernacle's eastern gate of entrance and with their coats removed the bodies of Nadab and Abihu from within the sanctuary of the Tabernacle. They had then taken the bodies outside of the camp and buried them.

The entire house of Israel had publicly mourned their loss at the tragic deaths of Nadab and Abihu. However, according to the commandment of the Lord, as priests, neither Aaron, nor his two remaining sons, Eleazar and Ithamar, could mourn publicly the deaths of Nadab and Abihu, for no priests were to mourn for the dead, or even touch them. Aaron had held his peace about the matter, but silently his heart and mind still reverberated with the remembrance.

The judgment of God irrevocably declared if any priest entered into the Lord's glory and presence, the priest must be in complete and total submission and reverence to the Lord's stipulations of dedication. Without exception. The Lord's sanctity would not allow anything less.

Because of the calamity that had occurred, the Lord had commanded a new ritual established for the Day of Atonement, along with further instructions with regard to what the Lord would require of any of his priests whenever they entered into the Tabernacle. The Lord's new instructions were very clear; if not adhered to in the minutest detail, any violator would die.

Henceforth, as the High Priest, only Aaron alone now had access into the court of the Holy of Holies to stand in the presence of the Lord. As the Lord's High Priest, his access into the most holy place would occur only once a year, and then not without the shedding of blood. The Lord's stipulations now required that as an offering for the atonement of sins for the priests, including the High Priest, and for the errors of the people, that specific blood was necessary. The blood of a young bullock for a sin-offering sacrifice and ram for a burnt offering sacrifice, and the blood of a goat for a burnt-offering sacrifice for the sins of the congregation of the people.

Aaron now nervously prepared to minister for the first time in his office of High Priest on this great Day of Atonement and begin the offering of the newly required sacrifices unto the Lord for the sins of himself, the priests, and the people of Israel. As he made his preparations, the vast encampment of the congregation of people waited, also nervously, and with great trepidation and silent suspense. They would not know if, unlike Nadab and Abihu, Aaron had correctly performed and fulfilled all of the Lord's requirements unless and until, alive, he had returned from within the Tabernacle.

Having donned himself in the seamless robe and priestly garments of pure white linen, with extreme care and deference, Aaron now began the order of the process for the Day of Atonement rituals.

Standing at the eastern door of the Tabernacle of the congregation, he presented two goats before the Lord, and taking the Urim and the Thummim, he cast lots for the decision of which goat he would offer as a sacrifice to the Lord and which goat would remain alive and loosed as a scapegoat into the wilderness.

This task accomplished, Aaron proceeded with the first order of the sacrifices. Selecting a bullock and killing it, he took the blood of the bullock and put it upon the four horns of the smoking brazen altar that stood within the Tabernacle's courtyard, offering the blood upon the brazen altar as a sin offering, making atonement for both himself and the priests.

Very carefully, Aaron next took a golden censer and scooped it full of burning coals from the fire of the brazen altar that perpetually burned before the Lord. With his hands full of sweet incense beaten very small, and carrying the censer, with cautious hesitation, he then entered into the Holy of Holies to stand before the clouded presence of the Lord.

Placing the golden censer of burning coals upon the pure gold lid of the Ark of the Covenant, also called the mercy seat, he dispersed the incense upon the burning coals, causing a sweet-smelling cloud of fragrance to cover the mercy seat and thinly spiral upward from between the outstretched wings of the golden cherubim.

Leaving the Holy of Holies, Aaron returned to the courtyard to the brazen altar to dip a consecrated basin into the blood of the slain bullock. Again, entering into the Holy of Holies to stand eastward before the mercy seat, he dipped his hand into the basin containing the blood of the slain bullock. With his finger, he sprinkled the mercy seat seven times with the blood of the sacrifice.

Having made atonement for the sins of himself and the priests, he now proceeded with the next sacrifice to offer for the sins of the congregation of the people of Israel. Selecting the goat upon which the lot had fallen to offer as a sacrifice to the Lord, Aaron slew it. Doing as he had done with the blood of the bullock, he took the blood of the slain goat and, carefully entering again into the Holy of Holies, with his finger, he sprinkled the blood of the sacrifice seven times upon the mercy seat.

So it was that the blood of a goat and a bullock covered the mercy seat of God. God's chosen representative and High Priest, Aaron, now humbly stood alone, with great apprehension, within the Holy of Holies of the Lord's Tabernacle.

Would the blood sacrifices he had now offered in the Holy of Holies be acceptable in the sight of the holy Lord God as a temporary yearly atonement for sin? As High Priest, had he properly performed his duties?

As High Priest of God's people, would he now be able to return to the congregation of his people, alive, from within the sacred Holy of Holies in the Lord's Tabernacle?

* * *

Heaven's entire host of angels waited in reverent silence and awe as they watched Jesus enter the eastern gate of the heavenly Temple of the Lord. Without hesitation, Jesus confidently proceeded into the sacred sanctuary of the Holy of Holies to stand before the presence of the Lord.

Risen from earth's grave, in complete and total submission and reverence to the Lord's stipulations of dedication, Jesus had endured the lowest of suffering and humiliation on a cruel cross of crucifixion to offer as sacrifice his life's blood and put away the sins of the entire world.

Clothed in the attire of High Priest, his once pure white and seamless linen tunic, now covered and dripping with the shed blood of his sacrifice, left a trail of bright red blood drops laying scattered upon the crystal sea of glass floor of the Temple of God.

Having no need to offer a sacrifice for *his* sins, for he was the spotless lamb of God, he had entered the Holy of Holies only to make one final and complete atonement for the remission of sins for the entire generations of God's people.

This atonement he now offered on the altar of heaven within the Temple of the Lord. Holding a consecrated basin containing his own shed blood, he dipped his hand into the basin, and with his finger sprinkled the heavenly mercy seat seven times with the blood of his sacrifice:

...the great drops of blood he had sweat as he agonized in the Garden of Gethsemane;

...the great drops of blood that had spattered in Pilate's hall of judgment as he took the thirty-nine stripes of a leather whip upon his bared back;

...the great drops of blood that had trickled down his body as the soldiers smote his face and plucked his beard;

...the great drops of blood that had flowed into his eyes and down his face as the crown of thorns had pierced his brow;

...the great drops of blood that had spurted as the Roman soldiers nailed his hands to the wooden crossbeam of the cross;

...the great drops of blood that had spilled and stained the foot of the cross as they pierced his feet;

...and the great drops of blood that had gushed forth when the Roman soldier pierced his side.

And so it was that as the Lord's spotless lamb, his blood now covered the mercy seat of God's altar in the heavenly throne room. As God's chosen representative and High Priest, Jesus stood with full confidence in that which he had now performed within the Holy of Holies in the Lord's heavenly Temple.

The seven sprinklings of blood sacrifice he had now offered in the heavenly Holy of Holies was indisputably acceptable in the sight of the holy Lord God as a permanent atonement for sin. As High Priest, he had properly performed his duties.

Once. And forever.

Triumphantly, as the High Priest of God's people, Jesus would now return to the congregation of his people, resurrected and alive, from within the sacred Holy of Holies in the heavenly Temple of the Lord.

* * *

And almost all things are by the law purged with blood; and without shedding of blood is no remission. It was therefore necessary that the patterns of things in the heavens should be purified with these; but the heavenly things themselves with better sacrifices than these. For Christ is not entered into the holy places made with hands, which are the figures of the true; but into heaven itself, now to appear in the presence of God for us: Nor yet that he should offer himself often, as the high priest entereth into the holy place every year with blood of others; For then must he often have suffered since the foundation of the world: but now once in the end of the world hath he appeared to put away sin by the sacrifice of himself. And as it is appointed unto men once to die, but after this the judgment: So Christ was once offered to bear the sins of many; and unto them that look for him shall he appear the second time without sin unto salvation.[10]

---

[10] Hebrews 9:22–28

CHAPTER 8

After these things Jesus shewed himself again to the disciples at the sea of Tiberias; and on this wise shewed he himself.

There were together Simon Peter, and Thomas called Didymus, and Nathanael of Cana in Galilee, and the sons of Zebedee, and two other of his disciples.

Simon Peter saith unto them, I go a fishing. They say unto him, We also go with thee. They went forth, and entered into a ship immediately; and that night they caught nothing.

But when the morning was now come, Jesus stood on the shore: but the disciples knew not that it was Jesus.

Then Jesus saith unto them, Children, have ye any meat? They answered him, No.

And he said unto them, Cast the net on the right side of the ship, and ye shall find. They cast therefore, and now they were not able to draw it for the multitude of fishes.

Therefore that disciple whom Jesus loved saith unto Peter, It is the Lord. Now when Simon Peter heard that it was the Lord, he girt his fisher's coat unto him, (for he was naked) and did cast himself into the sea.

And the other disciples came in a little ship; (for they were not far from land, but as it were two hundred cubits,) dragging the net with fishes.

As soon then as they were come to land, they saw a fire of coals there, and fish laid thereon, and bread.

Jesus saith unto them, Bring of the fish which ye have now caught.

Simon Peter went up, and drew the net to land full of great fishes, an hundred and fifty and three: and for all there were so many, yet was not the net broken.

Jesus saith unto them, Come and dine. And none of the disciples durst ask him, Who art thou? Knowing that it was the Lord.

Jesus then cometh, and taketh bread, and giveth them, and fish likewise.

This is now the third time that Jesus shewed himself to his disciples, after that he was risen from the dead.

So when they had dined, Jesus saith to Simon Peter, Simon, son of Jonas, lovest thou me more than these? He saith unto him, Yea, Lord; thou knowest that I love thee. He saith unto him, Feed my lambs.

He saith to him again the second time, Simon, son of Jonas, lovest thou me? He saith unto him, Yea, Lord; thou knowest that I love thee. He saith unto him, Feed my sheep.

He saith unto him the third time, Simon, son of Jonas, lovest thou me? And he saith unto him, Lord, thou knowest all things; thou knowest that I love thee. Jesus saith unto him, Feed my sheep.

—John 21:1–17

THE HEALER

The disciples were very worried about Peter. Usually impetuous and boisterous, Peter had spiraled into a deep, silent depression. He had been this way for weeks now, and it was beginning to seem there was nothing they could do to help him. Commissioned earlier, by the resurrected Lord Jesus Christ, to go and preach the gospel of good news to all nations, the disciples were eager to begin their commission. However, Peter adamantly refused to go with them. He did not consider himself worthy of the position "disciple," nor worthy to be included in the great commission to go and preach the gospel of good news.

It was not that Peter did not believe in the risen Lord Jesus Christ. Oh, he believed in Jesus with a certainty. He and the other disciples had seen Jesus twice now since the resurrection, all having witnessed that, indeed, Jesus *was* alive. And, on both occasions, as Peter stood at a slight distance apart from them, he had watched as they gladly and joyfully received and accepted everything Jesus spoke to them.

Peter had truly rejoiced for Jesus, and also for his fellow disciples, but not for himself. He had purposely stood outside the joyful circle that both times had gathered around the resurrected Jesus because there was something Peter had discovered he simply could *not* do. Ashamed and racked with guilt, he had not been able to look Jesus in the face. Moreover, neither had he been able to accept Jesus had intended that he, Peter, was to be included in the great commission. No, not after the terrible deed he had committed on the night before the crucifixion and death of his beloved Jesus.

Peter, shrouded in guilt and depression ever since that awful night, was not the man he had once been. Because he had confided in them as to what he had done on that night, the other disciples were fully aware of the cause of Peter's guilt and depression. They had all tried to reassure Peter that if Jesus had not meant to include Peter in the great commission, he certainly would have said so. After all, Jesus had never been one to mince words or fail to confront an issue when it was needful.

However, nothing they had said to try to reason with Peter had had any effect in pulling him out of his darkness of mind. Peter's repeated reply had been they just did not fully understand the enormity of what he had done. After all, *they* were not the ones that had afterward seen the look on Jesus' face that dreadful night.

No amount of arguing or attempts to console him had been able to persuade Peter any differently. Peter had even gone so far as to tell them all just leave and go on without him because it seemed obvious, they alone were the only true disciples Jesus had ever had, not him. He had then refused to speak of the matter anymore with any of them.

For days since, as they had all sat close by, Peter, not able to eat or sleep, had done nothing but sit silently by the shore of Galilee, staring out to sea. However, go on without him they would not do. Even though they had not been able to minister to Peter and did not know what else to do, they had decided they were going to stick closer to him than a brother. They loved Peter, and collectively, had made-up their minds they were not going to abandon him.

Therefore, the day before, when Peter had suddenly jumped up and announced to them that he was going fishing, it had appeared to them maybe Peter was finally coming to his senses. The fact he had wanted to do *something* had seemed encouraging. Thomas, Nathanael, James and his brother John, along with the two other disciples who were also there with Peter, had all zealously stated they too would go fishing with him. Everyone had immediately followed Peter into the boat before he had had a chance to change his mind.

It had been a long while since using Peter's fishing boat, so nothing more said, they all set about busying themselves with checking the boat's wooden hull for any leaks, and with inspecting the boat's large, triangular sail still attached to the central mast. They also made certain the boat's fishing net had ample stone weights attached to its edges.

Assured all was in order to set sail, they had then rowed a short distance from the shore and settled down to wait silently and patiently, hoping to catch sight of a shoal or school of fish that Peter could drop his net over.

The evening's sun had set without a single sight of any fish. As the long night had progressed, the disciples had silently prayed for the Lord to allow Peter to catch something. Anything! Their only concern that night was for Peter. The disciples did their best to give Peter positive words of reinforcement, enthusiastically stating to him that surely a prosperous fishing night lay ahead. But as the morning dawned, they inspected the fishing nets and it was evident the entire venture was without gain. Peter had caught nothing. Absolutely nothing. The disciples and Peter were dumbfounded.

Now bathed in the warmth of the spring morning, the small fishing boat idly floated upon the shallow, still waters of the Sea of Galilee, lazily drifting homeward toward the shore. With his back to the shoreline, the big, burly Peter sat hunched over with his elbows propped upon his bare knees, his fist clenched under his bearded chin, just staring glumly ahead. He had not spoken a single word since they had entered the boat the day before.

Though the early morning's sky was clear and bright, Peter's frame of mind was not. Although the previous night's failure was bad enough, the memory of a different past night was now torturing and taunting him...memory of the last night he spent with Jesus before the crucifixion. His mind reeled back, hauntingly, to replay the scene, forcing him to relive the memory afresh...

* * *

73

In darkness of night, bound by the captain and officers of the Jews, accompanying soldiers hurriedly took Jesus to the palace of the high priest, Caiaphas. Peter and another disciple followed, surreptitiously, from afar. Arriving just outside the palace, Peter stood without the palace's outer courtyard, cautiously observing. When the soldiers quickly took Jesus inside the palace, the other disciple, known by the high priest, also gained permission of entrance with Jesus inside the palace.

Shortly thereafter, the other disciple returned to speak to a woman keeping watch at the outer courtyard door of the palace. Reassuring her that Peter was just an innocent bystander and needed inside the inner courtyard, Peter was also able to enter. However, as Peter passed by the woman at the courtyard door, she gave him a long, shrewd stare. A few seconds later, a cold look of contempt crossed her face, and she then asked him, accusingly, if he was also a disciple of Jesus. Afraid for his life, Peter replied with a lie, the first of three lies he would tell that night, by curtly denying he was a disciple. He continued to walk swiftly inside, desiring to get as far away from her as possible.

Once within the palace courtyard, Peter sighted Jesus, still bound, standing on the palace steps above him. It appeared Jesus was on trial before Caiaphas, for assembled with Caiaphas were Jewish scribes and elders.

Peter also noticed an unusual pungent odor wafting through the night's chilly air. Seeking the source, he discovered the odor of strong fumes originated from a charcoal fire built in the courtyard. A group of servants and officers, warming themselves, stood clustered around the charcoal fire, for it was a cold night. Hoping to eavesdrop and possibly find out what was happening to Jesus, Peter went to stand near the group of servants and officers who stood warming themselves at the charcoal fire.

Trying his best to act nonchalant and go unnoticed, Peter slowly sidled up closer within the group gathered around the fire. He stretched out his hands toward the fire to appear only to be concerned with warming himself. However, Peter could sense one of the servant girls in the gathered group studying him hard and earnestly, causing him to again feel very uneasy. The servant girl then pointed directly at him, blurting out to the others that she had seen him before, with Jesus. She was certain he was a disciple of Jesus.

Fear again surged within him and Peter quickly responded with his second lie of the evening. He replied by vehemently denying he even knew of Jesus. Although everyone in the group momentarily looked at him with suspicion, they said nothing more. Peter defiantly remained where he was standing within the group as if to confirm his innocence. Apparently, his attempt at innocence worked. The subject of his identity temporarily dropped.

Time seemed to crawl as Peter remained at the charcoal fire, patiently waiting for any news as to the status of the arrest of Jesus. However, a soldier who had just joined the group standing with Peter at the fire, introducing himself as a servant of the high priest, said that he was among those present earlier in the garden of Gethsemane to arrest Jesus. With confidence and boldness, he asked Peter a direct question. Was it not Peter he had seen with Jesus in the garden of Gethsemane?

Peter then told his third lie of the night by again denying he knew Jesus. Cursing, he further declared, swearing with an oath to God, he did not even know the man Jesus of whom they were speaking. Immediately, just as he was finishing his statement, Peter heard a cock crowing loudly. While the cock crowed, Peter looked away, up toward the palace steps. When he did so, he saw Jesus turn to look directly at him. It was only at that moment Peter remembered Jesus telling him earlier in the day that before the cock crowed, Peter would deny him three times.

As Jesus continued looking upon Peter, Peter tore his eyes from the all-knowing stare, and he bolted. Escaping from the palace courtyard, he ran wildly into the anonymous cover of darkness. When the darkness had fully blanketed him, with great heaving sobs he had then wept bitterly.

* * *

Having the pain of that remembrance once again gripping his mind and heart, hot shame burned and reddened his face. He realized he would never be able to erase the anguish of that memory. It incessantly mocked him, for there was no doubt, he *was* guilty. Guilty of cowardice and the faithless betrayal of the pure and faultless love of the Master. And yes, guilty also of denying the Son of God, Jesus the Christ. He would give anything to have a chance to go back and undo that night, but there was no way he could now. The deed was done.

It seemed apparent to Peter the memory of his past was going to follow him wherever he went, touching everything he did. Discipleship out of the question, he had thought he would be able to go back to his old, previous trade, commercial fishing. That was his decision when yesterday he had announced to the others he was going to go fishing. However, here he was this morning, a failure once again. He could not even catch fish anymore.

Interrupting his melancholy, Peter jumped when he heard a man from the shore behind him loudly questioning if they had caught any fish. Since his was the only boat out on the water this morning, the man was obviously addressing the question to him and the disciples with him. How humiliating! Was the entire world going to gawk endlessly at him, with even strangers perceiving he was a failure at everything?

Seeing no use in even replying or looking back to see who was inquiring, Peter did not respond. The disciples replied for him by answering no, they had not caught anything. The man on the shore called out to them to cast the net over the right side of the boat because they were going to find fish for a catch. Everyone looked questionably at one another, wondering what in the world was the man talking about. Nevertheless, since there would be nothing to lose in doing so, they cast the net over. And lo and behold, instantly the net was swarming with fish. There were so many fish, try as they might they were not able to pull the net into the boat!

James and John exchanged glances, then jubilantly whooped and jumped for joy, nearly capsizing the boat. They perceived there could only be one explanation for this miracle, for this had happened only once before to them and Peter, nearly three years earlier. Grabbing Peter by the shoulders, John exclaimed, "That man on the shore is Jesus!"

Absolute panic and terror smote Peter's heart when he realized it had to be true that the man *was* Jesus. What was the matter with these disciples? When would they ever get it through their thick heads that Jesus being near-by was the last thing he wanted to hear? He had to escape and get away from all this madness! However, this time there was no darkness of night to cover his escape. Where was he to go?

His old, spontaneous nature surfacing, he did the first thing that came to his panic-stricken mind. Grabbing his outer fisherman's coat and girding it quickly about himself, he jumped overboard into the Sea of Galilee, prepared to swim as far away from Jesus as he possibly could.

In their excitement at beholding Jesus, the remaining disciples did not even notice Peter's departure. They were too preoccupied with finding their seats and grabbing all the oars necessary to begin rowing the boat to shore. With the boat's overloaded fishing net greatly hindering them, nevertheless, they settled-in and began laboriously rowing the short distance to the shore to once again be in their Master's presence.

Peter, however, treading water before he began the long swim to the opposite shoreline, noticed the boat departing and he quickly realized the foolishness of his reckless action. So close to shore, it was obvious Jesus would more surely notice if he swam away, rather than swim toward the shore. And have Jesus notice him was not the desire of his heart. Ever so slowly, he began the dreaded journey, swimming in the same direction as the boat, toward the shore.

Peter, and the disciples in the boat, landed almost simultaneously upon the shore where Jesus was standing. Upon their landing, they saw Jesus had a breakfast for all of them of fish grilling upon a fire, with bread also to eat.

But there was something out of the ordinary that caused Peter's heart to stand still and his breath to catch in his throat. With his thoughts racing, all he could think was, "Please Lord Jesus, No!" For the pungent smell that now wafted through the morning's air was unmistakable. It was wafting from a charcoal fire upon which their breakfast was grilling.

Peter could only keep his eyes downcast as he heard Jesus ask them to bring to him the fish they had just caught. Jumping for any chance to avoid looking at Jesus, Peter immediately took the opportunity afforded him and went to draw the net from where it rested in the waters, still attached to the boat. Once he drew the net to the land, out of the corner of his eye he observed that Jesus was watching him. Wanting to avoid any personal encounter with Jesus as long as he could, he decided to count slowly all the fish within the net.

He carried out the task and, remarkably, he discovered the net had quite a catch…it had more fish than he had ever caught at any one time in his entire career and the net had not even broken! Why, returning to fishing, as he had previously decided, was obviously his calling in life. After all, before Jesus had entered his life, fishing *had* been the first love of his life.

Quickly glancing toward Jesus and the disciples, with much self-satisfaction in his voice, he excitedly announced to all that the net contained 153 fishes!

Extending his arm in a welcoming gesture, Jesus simply smiled and invited them all to come and partake of the breakfast he had prepared. Breaking the bread into individual portions for each of them, Jesus gave to everyone a serving of bread, and likewise of fish.

For the first time in weeks, Peter had his appetite back and was able to join enthusiastically in the continuity of life as he had once known it. He felt as if life might once again be good.

Standing near the charcoal fire, Peter finished his last bite of the meal. As Peter finished his breakfast, Jesus pointed to the net laden with the fish. Catching him off-guard, Jesus asked of him, "Peter. Is the love you have for *me* more than the love you have for these fish?"

Looking directly in the direction where Jesus was pointing, Peter looked at the fish in the net. And as he did, the self-satisfaction within him instantly deflated and he realized he had only been deceiving himself. Fish were not the heart of the matter and he and Jesus both knew it.

Squaring his shoulders, but still not able to look Jesus in the face, he kept his eyes on the net of fishes and answered Jesus with all the honesty he had within him. "Lord, you know I love you more than these fish."

Jesus gently replied to Peter if that was the truth, Peter was to do as Jesus had commissioned him earlier. Peter was to go and be his disciple.

Before Peter could protest, Jesus again addressed the issue at hand by tenderly asking him, "Peter, do you love me? If you love me as you say, remember that I called you to be a fisher of men, *not* of fish. I want you to be my disciple."

Humbled, and without any pretense, Peter responded with anguish, "Lord, you know that I love you."

Jesus asked of Peter a third time, "Peter, do you love me?"

That Jesus had again asked him that question for the third time, Peter's heart became overwhelmed with the grief and sorrow that had plagued him ever since the night he denied knowing Jesus only due to his fear and panic. He replied, "Lord, you know all things. You know that I love you!"

Walking over to where Peter stood, with infinite affection and tender mercy, Jesus lovingly put his arm around Peter's shoulder. With the greatest care and compassion, Jesus explained to Peter, "I want you to understand that to be my disciple, I am not requiring you must love me perfectly. I am only asking you to love me as you already do, just as you are. Be my disciple."

The reality of Jesus' unconditional love wrapped-up in his words and actions were like a healing balm to Peter's bruised and scarred heart. Standing *within* the joyful circle that now surrounded him and the resurrected Jesus, the tears Peter had before been unable to shed since that awful night now poured forth as Jesus wrapped both arms around him, gathering him closely to his heart. Healing, cleansing tears washed down Peter's face and splashed into his heart. His healed heart began to soar with elation as he realized Jesus and his fellow disciples had never abandoned him, but collectively, had all stuck closer than a brother to him.

As his tears subsided, Peter discovered there was something else he now wanted to do...he wanted to again look into the face of his beloved Jesus. Happily, he now did so. With the anguish of the memory of the deed committed that terrible night now erased, Peter simply rested in the all-knowing gaze of the pure and faultless love of the Master.

By recreating the failures, Jesus lovingly and carefully restored unto him that which Peter had past denied. In the past, while standing at a charcoal fire, three times Peter had denied his love for Jesus. Yet today, once again while standing at a charcoal fire, three times Jesus restored to Peter the opportunity to refute those denials. The memory of this moment was going to follow Peter wherever he went, touching everything he did.

Healed by the Master's touch, once again Peter would return to be a fisher. A fisher of men. After all, since Jesus had entered his life, fishing *was* the first love of his life.

* * *

The spirit of the Lord is upon me, because he hath anointed me to preach the gospel to the poor; he hath sent me to heal the broken-hearted, to preach deliverance to the captives, and recovering of sight to the blind, to set at liberty them that are bruised.[11]

---

[11] Luke 4:18

CHAPTER 9

Now the serpent was more subtil than any beast of the field which the Lord God had made. And he said unto the woman, Yea, hath God said, Ye shall not eat of every tree of the garden?

And the woman said unto the serpent, We may eat of the fruit of the trees of the garden:

But of the fruit of the tree which is in the midst of the garden, God hath said, Ye shall not eat of it, neither shall ye touch it, lest ye die.

And the serpent said unto the woman, Ye shall not surely die:

For God doth know that in the day ye eat thereof, then your eyes shall be opened, and ye shall be as gods, knowing good and evil.

And when the woman saw that the tree was good for food, and that it was pleasant to the eyes, and a tree to be desired to make one wise, she took of the fruit thereof, and did eat, and gave also unto her husband with her; and he did eat.

And the eyes of them both were opened, and they knew that they were naked; and they sewed fig leaves together, and made themselves aprons.

And they heard the voice of the Lord God walking in the garden in the cool of the day: and Adam and his wife hid themselves from the presence of the Lord God amongst the trees of the garden.

And the Lord God called unto Adam, and said unto him, Where art thou?

And he said, I heard thy voice in the garden, and I was afraid, because I was naked; and I hid myself.

And he said, Who told thee that thou wast naked? Hast thou eaten of the tree, whereof I commanded thee that thou shouldest not eat?

And the man said, The woman whom thou gavest to be with me, she gave me of the tree, and I did eat.

And the Lord God said unto the woman, What is this that thou hast done? And the woman said, The serpent beguiled me, and I did eat.

And the Lord God said unto the serpent, Because thou has done this, thou art cursed above all cattle, and above every beast of the field; upon thy belly shalt thou go, and dust shalt thou eat all the days of thy life:

And I will put enmity between thee and the woman, and between thy seed and her seed; it shall bruise thy head, and thou shalt bruise his heel.

Unto the woman he said, I will greatly multiply thy sorrow and thy conception; in sorrow thou shalt bring forth children; and thy desire shall be to thy husband, and he shall rule over thee.

And unto Adam he said, Because thou has hearkened unto the voice of thy wife, and has eaten of the tree, of which I commanded thee, saying, Thou shalt not eat of it: cursed is the ground for thy sake; in sorrow shalt thou eat of it all the days of thy life;

Thorns also and thistles shall it bring forth to thee; and thou shalt eat the herb of the field;

In the sweat of thy face shalt thou eat bread, till thou return unto the ground; for out of it wast thou taken: for dust thou art, and unto dust shalt thou return.

And Adam called his wife's name Eve: because she was the mother of all living.

Unto Adam also and to his wife did the Lord God make coats of skins, and clothed them.

And the Lord God said, Behold, the man is become as one of us, to know good and evil: and now, lest he put forth his hand, and take also of the tree of life, and eat, and live forever:

Therefore the Lord God sent him forth from the garden of Eden, to till the ground from whence he was taken.

So he drove out the man; and he placed at the east of the garden of Eden Cherubims, and a flaming sword which turned every way, to keep the way of the tree of life.

—Genesis 3:1–24

THE TEMPTATION

In the midst of the garden of their paradise, Eden, Adam and his wife ran playfully, caught up in the frolic of a new discovery. Near the vicinity of the tree of knowledge of good and evil, a newly blossomed flower had caught his wife's eye and she had plucked it from the stem to bring its exquisite beauty closer to her view. When she did, a most aromatic fragrance filled her nostrils, causing her face to beam with delight.

Noticing the delight that filled her countenance, extending his arm toward her, Adam asked his wife if he, too, could examine the flower. Gleefully, she began to offer the flower to Adam, but then she pulled the flower back and, in fun, ran from Adam.

With the merriment of their innocent laughter ringing in the air, she would run a little way, then turn and wait for Adam to catch up, all the while holding the fragrant flower just out of his reach. As he would close in on her, off she would lightheartedly run again.

Adam was once again about to catch up to her and, with gaiety, she turned to continue the game. However, this time their playful game did not proceed. Their attention became diverted when, simultaneously, their eyes beheld another sight.

Standing tall and majestic in colors stood one of the living creatures of the earth. It was the serpent and he was stunning to behold. Adam's wife had seen him many times before, but always from afar. Now, at a much closer distance, she noticed that there was a subtle difference about this particular creature. He had an aura about him. Even though the Father had previously given both Adam and his wife dominion over every living thing that moved upon the earth, something about the serpent today caused them to become uneasy and discontinue their lighthearted game. With caution, they stood still, proceeding no further.

What Adam and his wife did not perceive was that the serpent had a great hostility toward them, and toward God, the Father. But the shrewd serpent had masked his hostility well for he was intelligent, cunning, and sly. His hostility stemmed from the fact that he knew Adam and his wife had the authority to take dominion over him and all other living things that moved upon the earth. However, unlike all the other creatures, he considered it beneath *his* dignity to be under *any* authority. The very thought repulsed him.

Therefore, the serpent had begun to devise a plan. A plan that, he thought, would eliminate man's dominion over him forever. The plan would cause Adam and his wife to sin against God, therefore forfeiting the dominion that God had given them. In addition, as an added bonus, he knew they would also forfeit eternal life. His plan seemed faultless. Once he had finished contriving all the finer details of his masterful plan, the serpent had slyly smiled to himself.

Patiently, he had waited for the perfect opportunity. Now here it was. He had Adam and his wife right where he wanted them. The serpent smiled his most charming smile. His radiance and majestic beauty began to mesmerize and envelop the couple, persuading their sense of caution to vanish.

Both Adam and his wife returned his smile. Clasping hands, they now proceeded nearer to the magnificent serpent. As they came closer, the serpent casually leaned against the gigantic trunk of the tree of knowledge of good and evil and temptingly looked up at the appetizing fruit that hung plentifully from the heavily laden branches.

Adam stopped in his tracks. His hand clasped in his wife's hand caused her to come to a halt also. Adam was remembering. He was remembering that in the past, before the Father created his wife and gave her to him, the Father had told Adam never to eat of the fruit of the tree of knowledge of good and evil because in the day that he did, he would surely die. The Father had so severely stressed it to Adam that, after the Father brought Adam's wife to him, Adam had shared with her the Father's directive.

Now furtively glancing at his wife, Adam saw she had followed the serpent's gaze and that she, too, was looking and smiling at the forbidden fruit. Apparently, she was not remembering what he had previously told her about the Father's warning. Protectively, Adam put his arm around his wife, drawing her closer to himself.

Adam began wondering whether he should take dominion over this situation. But then again maybe he was just being over-protective. After all, neither he, nor his wife, had purposely set about to seek out the tree of knowledge of good and evil, or its forbidden fruit. Moreover, the serpent had never before given Adam any trouble or had ever tried to usurp Adam's authority over him. For that matter, not one living thing that moved upon the earth had yet *ever* intruded his authority, in any way. Therefore, uncertain as to what he should now do, Adam remained silent.

Noticing Adam's uncertainty, and that his wife was now hungrily staring at the forbidden fruit of the tree, the serpent slyly seized his opportunity. In a tone that was soothing and as soft as velvet, the serpent spoke to Adam's wife, saying, "It is obvious that you desire to taste of this tree's fruit. Let me assure you that the fruit is as delicious as it looks. But hasn't God told you that you cannot eat of any tree in the garden?"

Taken aback by the serpent's questioning of the Father's words, Adam's wife, redirecting her gaze from the fruit to the serpent, hastily and defensively replied, "We are allowed to eat the fruit of the trees in the garden. It is just the fruit of *this* tree, the tree of knowledge of good and evil here in the midst of the garden, that the Father has said, 'you cannot eat of, or even touch, lest you die.'"

Once the words were out of her mouth, however, Adam's wife nervously realized there was something about her reply that did not sound right. What was it exactly that Adam had told her the Father had said? Dropping her eyes to the ground, she tried to remember.

Now she remembered! The Father had not told Adam that he could not *touch* the fruit. He had only commanded that Adam could not *eat* of the fruit. *Oh well*, she thought to herself as she shrugged her shoulders, *it is but a minor detail. The serpent will never know the difference.*

However, the serpent *did* know the difference. His plan was going exactly as he had hoped it would. The serpent swayed in movement ever so slightly. It was a tactful maneuver, meant to cause Adam's wife once again to look at him, for he knew his beauty impressed her. It worked. He now had her full attention. Pulling himself up to his full height, so that he towered over her, he assumed an attitude of superiority.

To imply that, apparently, they had both misunderstood the Father's instructions, the serpent knew that now was the time to interject his lie. Continuing his conversation with her, he persuasively said, "You will not *die* if you eat the fruit of this tree. God meant that in the day that you *do* eat of this tree's fruit, it will only add to your intelligence, making you much wiser. You will have the added knowledge of knowing good and evil, and become as gods."

The serpent carefully scrutinized Adam's wife, watching for her reaction. The eyes of Adam's wife widened with the revelation, and the serpent was able to read her face with cunning accuracy. He knew she had fallen into his carefully poisoned trap, and he could barely refrain himself from hissing in sweet satisfaction.

Adam's wife was literally aflame with the poison of the serpent's insinuation. She began to calculate the new information that was now coursing through her mind. Glancing once again at the tree, it was now evident to her that its fruit was obviously good for food. And why should she and Adam not be able to be wiser, or become as gods, just like the Father? Impulsively, she hungrily reached up and plucked off a sample of the enticing fruit.

Examining it closely, she confidently concluded that since there would be nothing to lose by eating the fruit but only gain, she bit into the fruit with relish to savor its juicy tastiness and partake of its knowledge.

Turning to her husband who still stood silently by her side, she offered to Adam the remainder of the fruit in her hand. Following her example, he did eat of the fruit also.

As quickly as they had partaken of the forbidden fruit, indeed, wiser they did both become. Wise enough to understand that what they had done was evil, an expression and state of being that they had never, until this moment, understood or comprehended.

As Adam and his wife looked at one another, their innocence now lost, they also became aware that they were both naked and exposed. Shamed by both deed and their present state of being, they quickly set about to find a covering for their guilt and nakedness. Hurriedly, tearing leaves from a nearby fig tree, they clumsily fashioned the leaves into aprons to cover their nakedness.

Just as they were finishing, a cool evening breeze began to blow gently, and in the breeze, they heard the voice of the Father who was walking in the garden. The Father always came to visit them in the cool of the day to walk and talk with them in fellowship, and all the times before, Adam and his wife had so loved their visits with him.

However, this time they were afraid to face the Father. For even though they had thought they would be able to cover up the guilt of their disobedience by their own efforts with the making of their aprons of fig leaves, they now perceived that it had been in vain. As they looked upon their makeshift aprons, it was apparent that their transgressions were only the more obvious.

Frantically, doing the only other thing they could hastily think of, Adam and his wife hid amongst the trees in the garden, irrationally trying to seek refuge from the Father's presence.

Trembling within the cover of the trees, they heard the Father's voice calling, "Adam? Where are you?"

The Father was just a stone's throw away from where they were hiding. With resignation, Adam knew it was no use. They could not hide from the Father forever. They might as well surrender. Adam looked at his wife, and she, too, understood what they must do. Together they grasped hands, and still trembling, they stepped out from the cover of the trees to stand before the Father.

Adam confessed. Avoiding looking directly at the Father, with the words tumbling from his mouth, he spoke, saying, "When I heard you in the garden, I was afraid because I knew I was naked. So I hid myself from you."

Now, the Father, knowing all things, already knew Adam's wife had been deceived into eating the fruit of the tree of knowledge of good and evil. He knew Adam had not protected her from danger, as he should have. Moreover, the Father also knew that Adam had not only failed in the protecting of his wife, but he had also directly disobeyed the Father's command by his eating of the forbidden fruit. The Father now expected Adam to recognize and confess his failure and disobedience.

To encourage Adam to confess fully, the Father asked him, "Adam, how did you know that you were naked? Have you eaten of the tree that I commanded you should *not* eat of?"

Adam, hoping to avoid reproach, was only concerned with placing the blame for his sin on anyone but himself. He replied, "Well, I did eat of the fruit. But my wife, the woman that *you* created to be my companion, she gave to me the fruit of the tree."

The Father, putting Adam's retribution aside for the moment, redirected his gaze from Adam to the woman. He asked of her, "What have *you* done?"

Adam's wife, with her eyes downcast, replied, "The serpent deceived me, and I did eat of the fruit."

The Father turned to look at the serpent. The serpent, with a smirk across his face, was still arrogantly leaning against the trunk of the tree of knowledge of good and evil. He had been watching and listening to everything said, feeling quite pleased with himself and smugly triumphant. He thought himself to be untouchable.

He, however, was about to discover that untouchable he was not.

The Father now addressed the serpent. With vengeance, his voice blasting his wrath, he stated, "Because *you* have done this, you are now cursed above all cattle and beasts of the field. For all of eternity upon your belly you shall go, and dust you shall eat all the days of your life."

The Father paused for just a moment before he continued to deliver his final edict upon the serpent. Letting the serpent know clearly what his final judgment would entail, the Father stated with absolute finality, "Furthermore, I will put hatred between you and the woman, and between your offspring and her offspring. Your offspring shall overwhelm the heel of the woman's offspring, accomplishing a *momentary* victory. However, her offspring shall overwhelm, totally crush, and destroy the head of your offspring and accomplish an *everlasting* victory, forever reversing this calamity you have created.

In a thunderous voice, the Father evoked one last instruction to the serpent, commanding him, "Now! Upon your belly! Depart from me!"

Instantly, the serpent fell upon the ground, face down. The impact of his fall caused dust to swirl in his nostrils and down his throat, the taste gritty and dry. Attempting to voice defiance, the serpent found he no longer had the ability to speak and converse. Writhing in defeat upon his belly, no longer triumphant, the serpent slithered away as fast as he could, all the while hissing with bitter dissatisfaction.

Having dismissed the serpent, the Father turned again to Adam's wife and instructed her, "Because of your disobedience, I will greatly increase your pain and sorrow when you conceive and bear children. And from now on, your consideration will be first to your husband, not yourself, and he is to be the head over you."

Finally, addressing Adam's retribution, he said to Adam, "Because you listened to your wife, not me, and ate of the fruit of the tree which I commanded that you should not eat, in sorrow shall you now till the ground. No longer will it bear its yield of vegetables and fruit to you without struggle. Instead, you will find thorns and thistles to hinder you when you search for a harvest. In toil and sweat only will you be able to eat, until the day that you return to the ground. No longer will you live forever. For out of the dust of the ground I formed you, and to the dust of the ground you will return when you die."

Adam hung his head in shame and disgrace. His wife, who Adam had now given the name Eve, began to cry softly. The magnitude of their guilt, and sin, seemed more than they could endure. And no longer live forever, but eventually face death and die? The penalty and punishment seemed more than they could bear. Now, even more, they still could not look at one another, much less the Father.

As the Father looked upon them both, tears began to fill his eyes. His compassion for them overwhelmed him within, and it felt as if his heart would break, for the Father did still so love them. Making a way, temporarily, to cover their guilt, shame, and sin, the Father took one of the innocent beasts of the field and shed its blood. And from the shedding of the innocent blood, the Father made coats out of the beast's skin. He then took the coats and with infinite tenderness and mercy, he gently clothed Adam and Eve, reassuring them that it was out of his love for them that he was providing their covering.

The Father again spoke, as though thinking aloud. "Behold, Adam has now become as one of us, knowing good and evil. Now, if Adam and Eve should take it upon themselves to eat also of the tree of life, they will live forever in their fallen state of disobedience. I must remove them from the garden where they have access to the tree of life."

And so it was, because of the great love that the Father still had for mankind, the Father expelled Adam and Eve from the Garden of Eden, removing them from any opportunity to partake of the tree of life.

To completely ensure and prevent them from returning to Eden, the Father took further action. He placed his Cherubims, his heavenly beings, eastward at the entrance to the Garden of Eden. At the Cherubims' disposal was a flaming sword that turned in all directions, guarding the entrance so that neither Adam nor Eve would ever again have possible access to the tree of life in the midst of Eden.

However, the loving Father was not leaving fallen mankind hopelessly in their state of sin for all eternity, void of any possible future redemption. For the Father had designed a plan. A plan that, he knew, would eliminate the fallen state of mankind forever. A future plan that would allow any person, if they so chose, eternal redemption by the Father from sin, therefore forfeiting the calamity the serpent had caused. In addition, as an added bonus, he knew mankind would once again then have the opportunity to inherit eternal life. His plan was faultless. Once he finished designing all the finer details of his masterful plan, the Father had wisely smiled to himself.

Patiently, he was waiting for the perfect opportunity...

* * *

Jesus, the last Adam, was returning from the wilderness in power and in strength. He had just successfully completed the first stage of commission from the Father. He had followed and obeyed, with complete and unwavering obedience, the commencement of the Father's plan of redemption for all of mankind.

The first Adam, in the Garden of Eden, had succumbed to temptation, disobeying the Father's instruction. In yielding to temptation, he had thereby forfeited all dominion the Father had given him over the earth and its creations, along with the loss of eternal life. He had fallen in sin, losing everything, both for himself and for all of future mankind.

However, where sin had abounded, the Father's grace had much more abounded. Jesus, the last Adam, had just resisted and overcame the devil's temptations and lies.

Soon, he would totally crush and destroy the head of Satan, thereby initiating the Father's restoration process for all of mankind. A plan that would allow any person, if they so chose, eternal redemption by the Father from sin, thereby reversing the calamity that the serpent had long-ago created. Once he had finished fulfilling all the finer details of the Father's masterful plan, Jesus, the last Adam, would provide an everlasting victory through the shedding of his innocent blood for the remission of mankind's sin.

Patiently, he was waiting for the perfect opportunity planned for death to be swallowed up in victory. Jesus, the Redeemer, would then only ask one thing of the Father...to see the Father's triumphant smile.

* * *

We follow this sequence in Scripture: The First Adam received life, the Last Adam is a life-giving Spirit. Physical life comes first, then spiritual—a firm base shaped from the earth, a final completion coming out of heaven. The First Man was made out of the earth, and people since then are earthy; the Second Man was made out of heaven, and people now can be heavenly. In the same way that we've worked from our earthy origins, let's embrace our heavenly ends.

I need to emphasize, friends, that our natural, earthy lives don't in themselves lead us by their very nature into the kingdom of God. Their very "nature" is to die, so how could they "naturally" end up in the Life kingdom?

But let me tell you something wonderful, a mystery I'll probably never fully understand. We're not all going to die—but we are all going to be changed. You hear a blast to end all blasts from a trumpet, and in the time that you look up and blink your eyes—it's over. On signal from the trumpet from heaven, the dead will be up and out of their graves, beyond the reach of death, never to die again. At the same moment and in the same way, we'll all be changed. In the resurrection scheme of things, this has to happen: everything perishable taken off the shelves and replaced by the imperishable, this mortal replaced by the immortal. Then the saying will come true:

"Death swallowed by triumphant Life!

Who got the last word, oh, Death?

Oh, Death, who's afraid of you now?"

It was sin that made death so frightening and law-code guilt that gave sin its leverage, its destructive power. But now in a single victorious stroke of Life, all three—sin, guilt, death—are gone, the gift of our Master, Jesus Christ. Thank God!

With all this going for us, my dear, dear friends, stand your ground. And don't hold back. Throw yourselves into the work of the Master, confident that nothing you do for him is a waste of time or effort.[12]

---

[12] 1 Corinthians 15:45–58 (The Message)

CHAPTER 10

Now the feast of unleavened bread drew nigh, which is called the Passover.

And the chief priests and scribes sought how they might kill him; for they feared the people.

Then entered Satan into Judas surnamed Iscariot, being of the number of the twelve.

And he went his way, and communed with the chief priests and captains, how he might betray him unto them.

And they were glad, and covenanted to give him money.

And he promised, and sought opportunity to betray him unto them in the absence of the multitude.

—Luke 22:1–6

THE FRIEND

His secret hoard of silver coins melodiously jingled as Judas let a handful of them run through his fingers. Having quietly slipped away in the dark cover of the night, far away from Jesus and the eleven other disciples, Judas had gone to check on the concealed stash of money. He had shallowly buried his secret stash in a worn leather pouch under an old gnarled olive tree, high atop a steep cliff. The pale light of the full moon sifted through the twisted branches of the ancient tree, glinting off the silver of the coins as they trickled back into the bag.

Miserly, in both character and deed, Judas allowed himself the luxury of a smug half-smile. His scheme was going precisely as he had planned. Soon, he should have enough money to get out on his own in comfort and begin personally to pursue amassing the fortune of which he had always dreamed. Exactly how he would accomplish his mission he did not yet know. But something would turn-up. Of that, he was certain.

As far back as he could remember, he had always yearned to be free from poverty. The years of his youth had been difficult. Born the destitute son of Simon Iscariot, there never seemed to be enough of anything. With scarcity of just the necessities, he had gone to sleep on many a night with hunger gnawing and growling within his empty stomach. During the daytime, he had spent much of his existence not in play, but in continually seeking to alleviate his never-ending hunger, daily hunting for scraps of food he could steal from the open market square inside the city gates of Kerioth. Consequently, while but a youth, he had determined poverty was a curse he would one day overcome by any means he could.

He had left his hometown of Kerioth in his early teens, searching for a means to acquire the wealth he so desired. Traveling afoot, he had drifted northward. Stopping at various towns that bustled with activity and the hope of prosperity, he had managed to acquire only odd jobs of manual labor for meager pay or barter. It had kept him fed and clothed, but little else.

Several years of this meager existence had passed when it occurred to him maybe he should seek to learn a trade. With youthful optimism, he began to inquire of merchants as to where he might possibly find an opportunity of acquiring a position as an apprentice. In no time at all, it seemed, he did have the opportunity of apprenticeship, for there was always a need for eager, youthful, and energetic workers in most professions of trade.

At first, it had seemed a profitable idea. In the course of the pursuant years, he had apprenticed for several tradesmen at various occupations. He tried his hand at carpentry, but soon discovered hewing down trees and then having skillfully to produce acceptable work with very crude tools was backbreaking, exacting, and laborious. He then ventured into leatherworking, but the foul smell of the dog manure used in the tanning process of the hides, the smell of which also infiltrated into his own skin, had repulsed him. His next endeavor had been masonry. He had found having to cut huge foundational blocks from a limestone quarry, hauling stones, and digging foundation ditches in the hot blazing sun were not pleasant tasks either.

Attempting to learn these various trades had been a slow and tedious process. A process for which he ultimately decided he did not have the time or the patience. He had concluded there must surely exist an easier way to prosperity.

The long, futile years he had spent in his quest to gain the security of wealth had taken their toll on him. Somewhere along the road of becoming a man, he had lost his youthful optimism and enthusiasm. His mind continually stayed on obtaining his due place in life; a place where he would no longer have to labor and toil. A place where he would no longer have to worry and fret about the future or for the peace of mind that he believed copious amounts of money would provide. He had become a bitter and hardened man driven by the thought that if only he had enough money, he would then never have need of anything else.

Continuing to drift on, he eventually found himself in the Galilean area. It was literally ablaze with activity. It had certainly appeared if ever there was a place for a man to get ahead, Galilee was where he could achieve it.

Never much of one to socialize, upon his arrival, Judas had quietly mingled among the noisy crowds, keeping his ears open for any of the local gossip that could possibly afford him an easy break to make up for the years he had squandered in trying to earn a living. What he was really looking for was a way to become rich quickly. In addition, if he could find a way to do it without actually having to labor for it, so much the better.

One particular tidbit of gossip he had discovered permeating the atmosphere of the area was something about a religious teacher by the name of Jesus. It seemed everyone was preoccupied with any information they could obtain about him. He was causing quite a stir among the locals, and Judas had also found himself becoming increasingly curious in hearing more about the man called Jesus.

What had especially caught his attention was the rumor that grown men were actually abandoning their profitable livelihoods to become followers of Jesus. Why, it was even rumored that one of them had been a tax collector before he had quit his job! Judas knew tax collectors were of the powerful class of the wealthy. Tax collectors were notorious for demanding, and collecting, exorbitant amounts of money from the residents and merchants so they could make huge profits from the excessive amounts they charged.

Judas had surmised if all he had heard was true, then the rumors were definitely worth his further investigation.

It had not taken Judas long to find Jesus and his small band of followers. All he'd had to do was locate the great multitudes of people that ultimately pursued Jesus wherever he traveled.

For days thereafter, Judas followed them everywhere they went, scrupulously observing all said and done. He had found the rumors to be absolutely true. In addition, Judas himself had heard, with his own ears, Jesus make the statement that no one who believed his teachings should worry about what they were going to eat, or wear, or worry how they should get by, for Jesus himself would take care of them. To Judas' way of thinking, Jesus surely must have had very great wealth if he could promise so much, to so many. It was evidently the big break Judas had pursued his entire life! He had hardly been able to believe his good fortune.

For several days, Judas had mused about how he too might benefit from Jesus and, at the same time, make a nice profit. He had deduced that if Jesus truly possessed such great wealth, if he, Judas, could devise a way to pilfer secretly just a small amount of it, surely no one would notice. If he could just acquire access to the obviously unlimited funds of Jesus, it should be a very simple objective for him to accomplish.

Since it was public knowledge Jesus was in the process of choosing disciples and that he would apparently accept anyone who was willing to follow him and his teachings, Judas had concluded that to become a disciple of Jesus was his only logical solution. The stipulations Jesus required were but a minor hindrance as far as Judas was concerned. The teachings of Jesus were of very little interest to him. However, Jesus' money was of great interest to him. In addition, since he was a stranger to the Galilean area, Judas had reasoned that Jesus would have no way of really knowing what his true situation and intentions were.

Temporarily without a means of support or spare money, Judas would have nothing to lose, but everything to gain. Throwing all caution to the wind, he had deviously approached Jesus, declaring he was willing to give up everything he had to become a devoted disciple of Jesus.

Well, not only had Jesus welcomed him as a disciple, he had even appointed Judas as his treasurer when, after several months, Jesus had eventually noticed the keen regard and notable ability for finances with which Judas was gifted!

It had been three years now since Judas had been chosen as one of the twelve elite who traveled with Jesus as his constant companions. Judas had kept a low profile, hardly ever speaking, lest he give away his sole intention. The very few times he had spoken out had only been when he felt, as the treasurer, they had missed opportunity to add monies to their treasury bag.

As far as his role as a disciple had been concerned, he had successfully feigned an interest in the teachings of Jesus, not having much choice other than to listen to his constant ramblings-on about some fantasy kingdom Jesus was going to establish, and that everyone should love one another. There was no doubt in the mind of Judas that Jesus had good intentions, but in the real world, only a fool would actually believe such nonsense. In the real world, Judas had found, it was every man for himself.

Pertaining to the great wealth Jesus had claimed to possess, Judas had never actually seen large amounts of it at any one time. Nonetheless, since Judas had joined with Jesus, he had never experienced any lack. The finances he actually did have access to, as the treasurer, had been more than adequate to sustain them thus far, allowing Judas secretly to embezzle a little here and there, stowing it away in his secret hiding place.

And so it was that Judas, once again, had now crept away in the dark shadows of the night to add a bit more to his personal treasury. It was not a large fortune, but it was more than he had ever had in the summation of his entire life.

His intuition told him it would not be long before he would be resigning from his position as the treasurer, and a disciple of Jesus. His association with Jesus had been the most lucrative when he had initially joined with him. Although the popularity of Jesus was renowned among the common people, among the wealthy Jewish and religious leaders, jealousy and opposition toward Jesus were steadily peaking. There had even been rumors in Jerusalem that the Pharisees and scribes were probing to find a reason to hand Jesus over to the Roman authorities and have him executed.

If there was one thing Judas would avoid at all cost, it was opposition with the wealthy. After all, it was the ranks of the wealthy he one day planned to join. Hence, severing himself from the association of Jesus would soon be inevitable.

Reburying his precious bag of money, Judas remained in his squatting position and stealthily scouted the area to see if anyone was down at the foot of the cliff. Seeing all was quiet and no one had ventured near, he arose to a standing position and quickly wiped his hands on his outer tunic, squinting in the meager moonlight to make sure there was no residue of dirt on either himself or his garment, which might cause curiosity as to what he had been doing. He tamped the loosened soil of the stony ground with his foot to make it level. Very carefully, so as not to lose his footing on the steep terrain, he made his way down the cliff. When he reached the bottom of the cliff, he then swiftly moved to join Jesus and the disciples for a dinner at the house of Simon, the leper.

Within minutes, he arrived at Simon's house where there were already many people loudly gathered and milling around. Warily, he quietly blended in amongst them. Shortly thereafter, Simon invited everyone to take their place of seating for the evening's meal.

They had all just sat down to recline for the meal when Judas noticed a woman silently enter the room carrying an alabaster box of very expensive spikenard ointment. She glanced around the room, apparently looking for someone. When her eyes fell upon Jesus, she quickly went to him. Breaking open the seal of the alabaster box, she proceeded to pour its costly contents upon his head, anointing him, obviously, as a devout gesture of love.

Judas could not believe what he was observing. Did the woman not realize how wasteful she was being? Why, the cost of the ointment alone was worth more than a year's wages! Instead of wasting it, if she had donated it to Jesus, Judas would have been able to sell it for more than three hundred pence! He could not help but think of the appealing lump it would have made in his own personal treasury bag.

Without thinking first, Judas blurted out, "Woman, why on earth did you waste that ointment?" All attention in the room diverted to him, and shocked gasps escaped from many.

Oh, no! What have I done? Is it that transparent I had only my own personal interest in mind? How can I rectify what I have just done? His mind racing, he quickly came up with a remedy, and he pompously exclaimed, "As the treasurer for Jesus, I could have sold that ointment for more than three hundred pence and given it to the poor and the needy!"

There! he thought, as he made his recovery. *That ought to resolve my dilemma!*

However, Jesus spoke up, openly rebuking him. Sternly, Jesus directly asked of him, "Why are you always so overly concerned about the poor? The poor will always be around, and whenever you want, you may give to them. But you will not always have me with you. Do you not understand my death is imminent? This woman has just anointed my body for burial!"

Judas could feel the redness creep up his neck, steadily extending until it covered his entire face. Extremely embarrassed and publicly humiliated, he hastily arose from the table and fled from the presence of all the judgmental eyes that seemed to now penetrate to the very depths of his greedy soul. Without another word, he left the room to escape into the nonjudgmental darkness. He was so upset, he did not even notice he had uncharacteristically left behind the treasury bag of money he was usually so responsible with keeping.

After nearly an hour of just walking around aimlessly in the dark preoccupied with how he was going to salvage his pride, he suddenly remembered and realized Jesus had intimated he was about to die. His recent humiliation now fading, Judas found himself thinking that if that were true, then he himself would suffer a considerable setback because he had planned to collect more money from the treasury bag before he actually set out on his own. It now looked as though his former plans were about to be aborted.

The last words of Jesus kept ringing in his ears. Jesus, himself, had said that his death was at hand. Well, if that was the case, then maybe there could be one last profit made after all. He would have to hurry, while there was still time.

Judas went straightway to pay a visit with the wealthy chief priests, wasting not a valuable moment. The sand in the hourglass of fate was about to run out, and he was a driven man, trying to beat fate at its own game.

While on his way, he hastily came up with what he thought would be an acceptable deal with the chief priests. It was no secret the religious leaders wanted to get their hands on Jesus. But for various reasons, they had never been able to lay hold of him. Well, Judas was an insider that could give them the whereabouts of Jesus at any given moment. And he was going to let them know, in a most subtle way, he was more than willing to pass on to them, with a price, of course, the information they so desperately wanted.

The wealthy were always willing to use their money as a means to get their own way, and he was going to make sure they understood, without a doubt, that he himself was also a man cut of the same cloth.

Once he had arrived at their residence within the Temple at Jerusalem, he knocked loudly upon the ornate door. The door opened, and Judas quickly introduced himself, briefly explaining in a low, intimate voice that as the official treasurer for Jesus, he had felt compelled to pay them a visit. The chief priests gladly welcomed and ushered him inside. Congenially, they and Judas sat down in a friendly manner, all facing one another.

Wanting to ensure his future with these influential men, he then told them although he had been a disciple and treasurer for Jesus for three years, he had only just now realized what folly it was for him to have ever gotten involved with such a zealot. Judas told them that in analyzing the situation, he thought maybe it was time he moved on, disassociating himself from Jesus entirely.

Then, as if thinking to himself, Judas casually mentioned that even though he had given up everything to follow Jesus, he just might as well count his losses, get on with his life, and make a new start.

The chief priests quickly interjected, stating they would gladly be willing to give him some money to help provide for him a new start in life. However, before they did so, they would like just one little favor of him. They would like to know where they might be able to find Jesus and speak with him privately. They had just a few questions they wanted to ask him, away from all the noisy crowds and such.

Judas stalled, not wanting to appear too calculating or eager. He also needed more time to ponder his plan, needing to be certain he in no way would suffer any repercussions by striking an actual deal with these men. Cautiously, he answered by replying he would need a bit more time to give it some thought.

Judas arose from where he sat, indicating he was ready to depart. Smiling faces surrounded him and he left amidst much well-wishing and backslapping, promising he would get back with them soon about the matter.

The opportunity conveniently arose the next evening.

Judas and the eleven other disciples had gathered together with Jesus to partake of the Passover meal. The disciple John had the honor of having seating to the right of Jesus, with Judas assigned to sit to the left of Jesus. No sooner had they begun to eat when Jesus made the shocking and disturbing statement one of them eating with him would betray him.

Most in the room did not know or understand what Jesus meant by the remark, but obviously, by the tone of his voice, he was very serious. To the majority of the disciples, it was beyond their comprehension, whatever Jesus was alluding to, that any one of them could possibly betray Jesus in any way. Thus, the mood in the room became somber and quiet.

Judas kept his eyes downcast, but the other disciples became very grieved, and one by one, they began to sorrowfully ask of Jesus, "Is it I, Lord?"

Nervously, Judas listened while each disciple asked the question of Jesus. Instead of directly denying each one individually, Jesus just sat silently until eleven of the disciples had questioned him. Again, he only reiterated that it was one of the twelve eating with him that would betray him.

Judas pondered the situation. Could it be Jesus was aware of what Judas was personally contemplating with the chief priests? After much thought, he could not believe that Jesus would be able to have any knowledge of the matter. The men Judas had conspired with would not jeopardize the confidentiality of their proposition. They had too much to lose by doing so.

Judas concluded that Jesus must have been speaking of someone and something else. Apparently, Jesus had some *other* person in his midst who had decided to turn a traitor to his cause. That could be the only other possibility. Therefore, Judas had no more time to spare before getting back with the chief priests. His decision about when he should take action was clear. It would have to be tonight, as soon as the meal finished, and he could opportunely escape.

Now that he was reassured in his own mind of the anonymity of his clandestine meeting the night before, and not wanting his secret intention to be obvious by being the only disciple who had not questioned him, he knew he too would have to ask if Jesus thought he was the betrayer in his midst. Waiting until Jesus preoccupied himself with dipping his bread for a sop, he then asked of him, "Is it I, Master?"

Jesus answered only by replying, "You have said."

Taking the sop, Jesus handed it to Judas. When Judas received it, very quietly, Jesus said to him, "What you are going to do, do quickly."

The other disciples listening thought it not unusual what Jesus said to Judas. They naively assumed that since Judas was the treasurer, Jesus was simply sending him on an errand to purchase something else they needed for the feast, or that maybe Jesus wanted him to do some other errand.

Judas, himself, saw nothing questionable in the remark either. He just supposed Jesus had probably noticed his thoughts had been elsewhere most of the evening, and that he might as well dismiss Judas to take care of whatever was on his mind. Judas immediately took advantage of his dismissal and escaped, resolutely, into the night.

Judas lost no time in making his way to the chief priests to let them know of his decision, as he had promised. The chief priests once again eagerly received him, and Judas importantly stated to them that he could tell them where Jesus was going to be later in the evening, for he knew the ritual to which Jesus was accustomed. He then informed the chief priests Jesus would be retiring to the garden of Gethsemane, an orchard just outside of town, where he routinely went to pray at the end of the day.

The chief priests were delighted to receive the information but were also wary. They explained to Judas they had tried to converse with Jesus on many occasions, but he would have nothing of it. Therefore, to get Jesus to allow them to question him, they would most probably need to have a military escort to bring him to them. They intended no actual harm to Jesus, they added. It was just that they needed to make certain they would have absolute assurance of the opportunity for questioning Jesus.

The chief priests continued to explain to Judas that after he had visited them the night before, they had given the matter considerable thought. They had decided it would probably be best that Judas also accompany the military escort in order not to unduly alarm Jesus at their summons.

Having stated their intentions, they asked Judas if he would be willing to accommodate their request. And, of course, to remember they were more than willing to reimburse him monetarily for any inconvenience their request might cause him. The price of thirty pieces of silver should more than satisfy any inconvenience he might suffer; did he not agree?

Judas was not concerned about their pious intentions. His only concern was the compensation that was in it for him. He elatedly thought to himself that the amount of money they were offering him was a handsome amount indeed. Without further resignation, he quickly replied he was comfortable with the terms of the agreement.

Beaming with generosity, they graciously asked Judas to wait briefly while they made the necessary arrangements.

In the course of less than an hour, the chief priests returned with the promised thirty pieces of silver, and with information of the necessary military escort. A military cohort of more than six hundred soldiers and officers of the chief priests and Pharisees was awaiting him outside to accompany him to the garden of Gethsemane.

The thirty pieces of silver exchanged hands, and Judas pocketed the money handed over to him. They discussed a few more minor details and the transaction concluded.

Leaving the Temple's interior, Judas walked outside into the night to meet with the military band assigned to accompany him. The light of the lanterns and torches the soldiers held in their hands illuminated the night's darkness. It did not escape his notice that the soldiers were also carrying clubs.

The chief priests had earlier informed Judas the soldiers would have no way of knowing who they were to escort back to them. Therefore, it would be necessary for Judas to give the soldiers detailed instructions as to the elaboration of his contrived plan.

Introduced to the soldiers, Judas proceeded to explain to them that they would find Jesus in the company of eleven other men. However, the one whom they were to lay hold of, and be concerned with securing, would be the one that he, Judas, would walk up to and greet with a customary kiss.

Once he established the course of action to take, with Judas leading the way, he and the military band set out on their route. Judas led them to the garden of Gethsemane, noting exactly where Jesus was standing. Looking over his shoulder at the soldiers in the front ranks, he nodded. Drawing near to Jesus, in a loud voice all could hear, he warmly addressed him by saying, "Master!" He followed his greeting by cordially leaning forward with the traditional kiss.

As he leaned away from Jesus, Jesus looked at him fully, and solemnly asked, "Friend, why have you come here?"

Briefly, Judas became flustered. However, before he could fully grasp the meaning of what Jesus had said, the soldiers came forward, roughly laid hands on Jesus, bound him, and took him away. It happened so quickly, Judas had no time to reflect then on the enormity of Jesus' words. Judas watched as the soldiers marched away with their captive, their bobbing torches and lanterns soon fading into the night, leaving Judas with only the solitude of the darkness remaining as his companion.

Judas looked around forlornly. The other disciples that had been with Jesus had chaotically scattered when the soldiers took Jesus off into the night. Only Judas now remained. For the first time ever in his life, Judas found he did not welcome the isolation, or darkness. Because echoing in the darkness, reverberating in the hollowness of his heart, was the fact that Jesus had sincerely called him "friend."

It was a word of endearment Jesus had spoken lovingly. And if ever there was anything Judas knew, he knew Jesus did not use such terms lightly.

Until this moment, other than words of prospering financially, he had never really taken seriously any of the words of Jesus. Now, the reality of the fact that Jesus had considered him his "friend," he could not cast-off, or erase, from his blackened heart.

Reflecting upon his own selfish past, Judas now realized he had always used people for what he could get out of the relationship, never for what he could give. He, himself, had never been a true friend to anyone, least of all Jesus. Not once had he ever cared about Jesus, shown him any warmth or affection, or in any way expressed a desire truly to serve Jesus or his ministry. Yet Jesus had genuinely accepted and loved him anyway.

He at last realized, without a doubt, Jesus had willingly been the best, and only, true friend he had ever known or had.

Not once had Jesus ever doubted Judas or his capabilities, nor had he mistrusted Judas as his treasurer. He had never once asked Judas for an accounting of the finances he had allowed him to handle. Moreover, he could have demanded it of Judas, at any given moment. Nevertheless, without the slightest hesitation, he had entrusted Judas with all that he had.

Seeing the darkness of his past in the light of honesty, Judas finally knew what it was to feel guilt, and also be accountable for the depravity of the deeds he had committed.

Remorse filled his heart, mind, and soul. In the courtroom of his conscience, he could only stand guilty and convicted. It did not now matter the hand life had dealt out to him. His heart repented only for what he, himself, had dealt out.

The thirty pieces of silver given him for the betrayal of his one solitary friend now brought only tremendous torment to him. Was there *any* way he could rid himself of the guilt and shame?

The only thing he could think of was to return the money he had taken as payment for his betrayal of Jesus. The early morning about to dawn, he headed for the Temple where he had first encountered the chief priests with his initial proposal of treachery.

When he reached the Temple, he pounded heavily upon the door housing the priests' private living quarters. There was no answer. Despondently, he left with the thirty pieces of silver in the pocket of his tunic weighing down every step he took as he retreated into the dawning of the faint early morning light.

Judas sought a place to lay down his head but could find no rest. When the morning was fully come, Judas made his way back to the Temple and began to inquire of the many that were beginning to gather on the steps as to whether there was any word of what was happening to Jesus. He discovered Jesus was now in the custody of Pontius Pilate, the governor.

Listening to the various reports, he discerned it was only a matter of time, very little time, to be exact, before they delivered Jesus up for execution. Of that, there was no doubt. He saw with clarity what he had caused, and what was to be. He could no longer deny the fact he had known all along what the chief priests had really had in mind when they wanted to question Jesus; he could no longer deny the fact, ultimately, they had wanted Jesus condemned and executed.

Judas saw himself a condemned man also. *He* deserved it, for he was guilty. But not Jesus. Jesus was innocent and blameless, and the chief priests must be informed.

So again, he sought to find the chief priests to return their thirty pieces of silver and try to undo what he had initiated.

This time he did find them to be at the Temple. As they allowed him entrance, tearfully, he sobbed his confession to them that he had sinned, and betrayed innocent blood by betraying Jesus. He asked if there was any way they could see to the release of Jesus.

With not even a hint of their formerly warm receptions, the chief priests answered him by coldly replying, "And? What is that to us? That is *your* problem, not ours."

Under the stares of their icy contempt, Judas turned to retreat. As he turned, the pieces of silver in the pocket of his tunic loudly jangled. Reaching into his pocket, he withdrew the thirty pieces of silver and cast them down upon the cold marble floor of the Temple. Blinded by his tears, Judas did not notice, nor would he have cared, that the coins rolled with abandon in all directions on the vast expanse of the Temple's floor. All he cared about was ridding himself of his traitorous compensation.

Judas fled from the Temple. He had to get to his personal stash of money and rid himself, too, of its guilt. To those he passed on the journey to reach the privacy of his hiding place, he appeared to be a crazed person as he stumbled along, all the while still sobbing.

Reaching the base of the huge and misshapen old olive tree, stretched out on his belly, he began to claw demonically at the stony ground to unearth his personal money bag. When his bleeding fingers contacted the familiar leather, with fervor, he snatched the bag from its shallow grave. Undoing the narrow purse strings, he clumsily opened it. Extending his arm over the edge of the cliff, holding the bottom of the money bag, he turned the leather pouch upside-down, spilling its contents into the faraway, distant valley.

He waited for the flood of relief he so desperately desired. However, relief did not wash over him as he had thought it would and had expected. The blackness in his soul remained, relentlessly haunting and jeering at him.

There was nowhere else to go. He had no friend he could turn to for solace, for he had betrayed the one and only friend he possessed. Finding no consolation, hopelessly, he determined there to be only one other solution that would bring an end to his relentless torment.

He removed his outer tunic and using his teeth, he tore the linen into strips. With his still bleeding hands, he securely tied the frayed strips together into a single length. Picking up the discarded waist cord of his tunic, he fastened the two together to form one long rope. He then fashioned the waist cord end of the rope into a crude hangman's noose.

With the last reserve of strength his sleep-deprived body could muster, he pushed himself up to a standing position. Taking the loose, unknotted end of the makeshift rope, he weakly tossed it onto a low branch of the olive tree, overhanging the cliff. Leaning out over the cliff's edge, being careful not to look downwardly, he stiffly knotted it tightly around the thick limb, tugging on it to make certain it would hold.

Leaning back into the ledge of the cliff, he deliberately placed the noosed end around his neck. After adjusting it and pulling it snug, Judas closed his eyes and took one last deep breath before flinging himself from the cliff's edge. The momentum of his falling body caused his neck to snap as if it was but a twig.

Momentarily, his body hung and swayed, suspended in midair. But the weight of his body was too much for the old, brittle limb. It broke, sending Judas' body falling headlong into the valley far below.

* * *

After suffering the death of his mortal body on the cross for the sins of the world, the immortal spirit of Jesus immediately descended into the bowels of Hades. There, for three days and three nights, he privately warred with Satan, overthrowing and usurping Satan of all authority over death, Hades, and the grave. Stripping Satan of his power and crushing his authority, Jesus victoriously took from him the keys of death and Hades.

Having fully conquered Satan and his entire dominion and domain, Jesus was preparing to leave Hades and return to the earth. Resurrected from the grave, he would return for forty days to prove and announce his victory to the world, before ascending on high to sit at the right hand of his heavenly father.

But not before performing one final assignment.

For Jesus had also died to set the captives free. And deep inside the bowels of the earth, within a gated fortress, were an underworld of departed human spirits assembled together and locked up, held captive by Satan. A compartment of Hades, it contained only the repentant spirits of human beings whose earthly, physical bodies had suffered death.

Born from the time of Adam to Christ, these penitent captives' mortal bodies had suffered death before Jesus was able to die for their sins. They had not had the opportunity to acknowledge Jesus as their Savior and receive the gift of salvation. Due to the enduring mercy of the Lord God and having no legal right to do anything else with them, Satan was only able to hold them as captive prisoners. Among those confined within this compartment was one of his latest captives, Judas Iscariot.

However, the prisoners were about to receive the good news of the gospel through an uninvited visitor. One who was to permanently change the course of their bondage by delivering them from the power of Satan. Jesus, the Christ, son of God and son of Man, was about to inform and release the imprisoned captives of Satan. Forever.

Marching up to the prison gate and using the key he now possessed and held in his right hand, he unlocked it. Powerfully, he flung the gate wide open to reveal before him a seemingly endless sea of prisoners.

They stood before him meek and downtrodden, deeply distressed and brokenhearted, helpless prisoners held captive against their will. Their bleak, haunted eyes met his compassionate gaze with wonderment.

With the fullness of the Spirit of the Lord upon him, anointed, he triumphantly preached to the prisoners the good news of the redemption he had purchased for them. Moreover, not only had he redeemed them, but he was also taking them with him as he now ascended on high to the Father.

Having proclaimed his purchase of their liberty, he now stepped aside the opened prison gate, indicating it was time for their departure and freedom. Looking over his shoulder at one of the captives in the front ranks, he nodded.

The captive, Judas Iscariot, fell to his knees, and sobbing his uncertainty, asked, "Friend, why have you come here?"

Fully grasping the meaning of what Judas had asked, Jesus went to him and knelt down, gently placing his nail-scarred hands upon Judas's stooped shoulders.

Looking at him fully and solemnly, Jesus replied, "Come, let us reason together, and settle this matter once and for all. Although your sins were as scarlet, I have washed them whiter than snow. Because you repented, I have washed you and made you clean."

Rising from his bent knee to his full height, Jesus stood and held out his hand of redemption, lovingly, saying, "Friend, come."

Finally, Judas understood.

He *did* have a friend he could turn to for solace. And forgiveness. Moreover, there *was* somewhere else to go…a place where he would no longer have to labor and toil…a place where he would no longer have to worry and fret about the future or for peace of mind.

Judas stood, accepting the offered hand of redemption. At long last, Judas would never have need of anything else. He had found his new start in life. In Jesus.

* * *

Greater love hath no man than this, that a man lay down his life for his friends.[13]

---

[13] John 15:13

CHAPTER 11

Now a certain man was sick, named Lazarus, of Bethany, the town of Mary and her sister Martha.

(It was that Mary which anointed the Lord with ointment, and wiped his feet with her hair, whose brother Lazarus was sick.)

Therefore his sisters sent unto him, saying, Lord, behold, he whom thou lovest is sick.

When Jesus heard that, he said, This sickness is not unto death, but for the glory of God, that the Son of God might be glorified thereby.

Now Jesus loved Martha, and her sister, and Lazarus.

When he had heard therefore that he was sick, he abode two days still in the same place where he was.

Then after that saith he to his disciples, Let us go into Judea again.

His disciples say unto him, Master, the Jews of late sought to stone thee; and goest thou thither again?

Jesus answered, Are there not twelve hours in the day? If any man walk in the day, he stumbleth not, because he seeth the light of this world.

But if a man walk in the night, he stumbleth, because there is no light in him.

These things said he: and after that he saith unto them, Our friend Lazarus sleepeth; but I go, that I may awake him out of sleep.

Then said his disciples, Lord, if he sleep, he shall do well.

Howbeit Jesus spake of his death: but they thought that he had spoken of taking a rest in sleep.

Then said Jesus unto them plainly, Lazarus is dead.

And I am glad for your sakes that I was not there, to the intent ye may believe; nevertheless let us go unto him.

Then said Thomas, which is called Didymus, unto his fellow-disciples, Let us also go, that we may die with him.

Then when Jesus came, he found that he had lain in the grave four days already.

Now Bethany was nigh unto Jerusalem, about fifteen furlongs off:

And many of the Jews came to Martha and Mary, to comfort them concerning their brother.

Then Martha, as soon as she heard that Jesus was coming, went and met him: but Mary sat still in the house.

Then said Martha unto Jesus, Lord if thou hadst been here, my brother had not died.

But I know, that even now, whatsoever thou wilt ask of God, God will give it thee.

Jesus saith unto her, Thy brother shall rise again.

Martha saith unto him, I know that he shall rise again in the resurrection at the last day.

Jesus said unto her, I am the resurrection, and the life: he that believeth in me, though he were dead, yet shall he live.

And whosoever liveth and believeth in me shall never die. Believest thou this?

She said unto him, Yea, Lord: I believe that thou art the Christ, the Son of God, which should come into the world.

And when she had so said, she went her way, and called Mary her sister secretly, saying, The Master is come, and calleth for thee.

As soon as she heard that, she arose quickly, and came unto him.

Now Jesus was not yet come into the town, but was in that place where Martha met him.

The Jews then which were with her in the house, and comforted her, when they saw Mary, that she rose up hastily and went out, followed her, saying, She goeth unto the grave to weep there.

Then when Mary was come where Jesus was, and saw him, she fell down at his feet, saying unto him, Lord, if thou hadst been here, my brother had not died.

When Jesus therefore saw her weeping, and the Jews also weeping which came with her, he groaned in the spirit, and was troubled.

And said, Where have ye laid him? They said unto him, Lord, come and see.

Jesus wept.

Then said the Jews, Behold how he loved him!

And some of them said, Could not this man, which opened the eyes of the blind, have caused that even this man should not have died?

Jesus therefore again groaning in himself cometh to the grave. It was a cave, and a stone lay upon it.

Jesus said, Take ye away the stone. Martha, the sister of him that was dead, saith unto him, Lord, by this time he stinketh: for he hath been dead four days.

Jesus saith unto her, Said I not unto thee, that if thou wouldst believe, thou shouldest see the glory of God?

Then they took away the stone from the place where the dead was laid. And Jesus lifted up his eyes, and said, Father, I thank thee that thou hadst heard me.

And I know that thou hearest me always: but because of the people which stand by I said it, that they may believe that thou hast sent me.

And when he thus had spoken, he cried with a loud voice, Lazarus, come forth.

And he that was dead came forth, bound hand and foot with grave clothes: and his face was bound about with a napkin. Jesus saith unto them, Loose him, and let him go.

—John 11:1–44

THE TEARS

Jesus and his disciples were abiding just beyond Jordan in the village of Bethabara when a breathless messenger from the town of Bethany, about eighteen miles away, hastily approached them. Two days earlier, Mary and her sister Martha had dispatched the messenger to bring a most urgent message.

The messenger came to an abrupt halt, stopping just mere feet in front of Jesus and the disciples. Attempting to catch his breath, the messenger was momentarily speechless. After swallowing several gulps of air as he wiped the beaded sweat from his brow, he then panted out, "Lord, you need to know that Lazarus, whom you love dearly, is sick and very weak." Silently, he hoped he was not too late. According to Mary and Martha, the life of their brother was fading fast. And that had been two days ago!

The disciples had looked around at one another, wondering how Jesus would respond to the message. They all knew how much Jesus loved Mary, Martha, and Lazarus. Why it had not been that long ago that they all had last eaten in fellowship with one another. Lazarus had seemed fine at the time, a perfect picture of health. How could this be? They anxiously awaited to hear how Jesus would reply.

Jesus, however, had not been anxious or alarmed by the message. For two days earlier, while in prayer with his heavenly Father, he had received information of Lazarus and his condition of health. Already knowing what the outcome of the situation would be, Jesus simply stated to all present and waiting for a reply that the sickness concerning Lazarus would not bring death to Lazarus, but would bring glory to God, afterward bringing glory to the son of God.

Collectively, everyone had breathed a sigh of relief. The messenger had then departed to return to Bethany to give Mary and Martha the good news. Jesus and his disciples had continued to abide at Bethabara, resuming their ministry.

However, Jesus stunned his disciples when two days later he informed them that he wanted to leave Bethabara and return to Judea. It was just several weeks earlier that they had barely escaped from Solomon's porch at the Temple in Jerusalem when the Jews attempted to stone Jesus for blasphemy by claiming to be one with the Father. Not understanding his reasoning to return back to Judea, his disciples had incredulously inquired of their Master if he was crazy. Why, the Jews had tried to kill him when he was last there! And he wanted to go back?

As always, Jesus proceeded to state to them that if they continued to look at circumstances as they appeared in the natural, they would stumble, just like a man trying to walk in the dark without any light. But if they would remember that in Him there was no darkness, because he was the light of the world, then in following him, they would not stumble over the appearance of what their natural eyes saw.

Seeing the confused looks on their faces and knowing they did not understand what he already knew, he gently told them his reason for needing to return to Judea. He reminded them of the messenger that two days earlier had brought the report of Lazarus. As they were remembering the event, the disciples all nodded their heads in acquiescence, waiting for Jesus to continue. Jesus continued his explanation by telling them that their friend Lazarus was asleep and that he, Jesus, needed to go wake him up.

Bewildered, the disciples asked him why he would want to do that. If Lazarus was sleeping, he obviously needed his rest.

Realizing his disciples were becoming only more confused and not understanding a word of what he was trying to tell them, he then spoke plainly of what their natural eyes would see when they returned to Judea. Lazarus was dead.

The disciples had been speechless with shock. Just two days before, Jesus had told them all that the sickness concerning Lazarus would not bring death. Then just minutes ago, Jesus had told them Lazarus was asleep. And now Jesus had told them that Lazarus was dead? Could the man not make up his mind? Had Jesus been in the sun too long? And what had all that talk been of about not walking in the dark, but to walk in the light? If ever anyone had needed advice about not being in the dark about matters, it certainly sounded like their Master was the one that needed the counsel! He had made absolutely no sense at all to them. Would they ever understand this Jesus?

The only reply Jesus gave was that all things were being accomplished in the manner that they were with the intention of causing them to believe. It did not matter how they perceived the situation. They were all going, nevertheless, back to Judea.

Dejectedly, one of his disciples, Thomas, spoke-up. With weary resignation in his voice, he addressed his fellow disciples by saying that they all might as well be ready to go back to Judea prepared to die with Jesus.

Jesus said nothing further to them. He knew they would have more than enough to think about as they journeyed the next two days back to Judea. They would realize soon enough all of which he spoke.

When they had reached Bethany in Judea, Lazarus, already buried on the day of his death, was now in the grave four days. At the cemetery, just outside of the city limits, many Jews had started to arrive to go to where Lazarus was buried. According to the custom of the day, they believed that after three days, the spirit of the deceased left the body, thus causing corruption of the corpse to begin on the fourth day when decomposition took place. Therefore, the many mourners were going to gather at the gravesite with much weeping to grieve loudly for the departed spirit of Lazarus.

One of the Jews on his way to the sepulcher of Lazarus, noticed the arrival of Jesus and his disciples as they were approaching the cemetery. When he saw this, he instead ran straightway to Mary and Martha's house to inform them that Jesus had finally arrived.

When Martha had received the news, she had gone to meet Jesus to speak with him. Martha, having always been the assertive one of the family, had made-up her mind that she was going to confront Jesus as to why he had not rushed to their rescue and prevented the death of her brother, Lazarus, whom Jesus had professed to have loved so much. Mary, however, had remained at home.

Martha had found Jesus just outside the cemetery. She marched right up to him, and with accusation dripping from her voice, she bluntly stated to him that if he had been around when they needed him, her brother would not have died. She had not cared who else heard her, she was so angry. But once the words were out of her mouth, with chagrin, she had tried to soften her accusation by stating that even at this moment she still knew that whatever Jesus asked of God, it would be given to him.

Seeing beyond Martha's hurtful, stinging words, and knowing the grief of her heart, Jesus had tried to console her by stating that he was going to resurrect Lazarus.

Not fully grasping the meaning of his statement, Martha replied that she knew that on the day of redemption that her brother would be resurrected.

Still trying to get Martha to look beyond her grief and the evidence of what her natural eyes were seeing, Jesus had reminded Martha, for she had heard his teachings many times before, that he himself was the resurrection and life, and whoever believed in him, even if they died a natural death in the body, they would continue to live. He had then asked her if she believed what he was saying.

Martha, however, still had not understood the fullness of his words. She had replied only that she did believe that he, Jesus, was the anointed and prophesied son of God. Secretly though, Martha felt she obviously was not getting anywhere with her chastisement of Jesus. Why would he not just admit that it was his fault that Lazarus had died? If he truly loved her, or Lazarus too for that matter, he would not have allowed any of this to happen.

Leaving the scene, Martha had marched herself right back home. She knew someone that Jesus would listen to. Someone that could pull that head of Jesus out of the clouds and get him to face reality. Someone that could get him to admit that he was the cause of their family's grief by letting them all down. Why, a miracle would have been nothing for Jesus to have performed! She had seen him heal plenty of other people. But no, he had had more important things to do. Like lollygagging around, and then showing up four days late for a funeral. Oh yes, she knew the person that could bring him down a peg or two.

Arriving at her destination, upon entering her house, she had to push through the many loudly weeping mourners so that she could go straight to her sister's room. But once inside, she found even more of the mourners clustered around Mary. Grabbing Mary's hand, she pulled Mary aside to herself to talk to her privately.

Whispering, so that no one else could hear her, she had then informed Mary that Jesus was, indeed, just outside of town at the cemetery and that he had asked for Mary. Mary's tired face had it up like a lantern, and she darted out of the room to run to Jesus. Abashed, Martha hope she had done the right thing after all.

Noticing how quickly Mary had left, all of the gathered mourners within the house followed after her, assuming that she was going to go to mourn at the gravesite of Lazarus. Martha followed closely behind.

When Mary met Jesus, overwhelmed with her grief, she fell prostrate before him weeping, and she too cried that if only he would have been around when they needed him, Lazarus would not have died.

As Jesus looked at Mary and the Jews all loudly weeping, it was at that moment that a then nameless and disguised spiritual darkness crept close by. Jesus began to waver, causing the spiritual light that was within him to dim ever so slightly. Taking its cue, the darkness began to creep closer toward Jesus, blending in the sobbing, grief, and disappointment.

Feeling very weary, Jesus sighed with heaviness of heart. He then asked in which sepulcher would they find Lazarus buried. They had proceeded to take him through the tombs to show Jesus in which one they had placed Lazarus.

Winding their way through the various natural caves used for burying the dead, surrounded by death on all sides, Jesus remembered the purpose for which he had come to earth. To die.

Soon, he too would be involved in such a scene as this. But instead of being on the outside of a tomb with a stone rolled in front of it, he would be on the inside, lifeless, in the unknown darkness of death.

Crouched and waiting in ambush, still lurking in the shadows, the creeping darkness watched Jesus' outward slump of weariness. Quickly, it then spread; permeating the entire cemetery, causing the weeping gathered mourners to wail even louder. As Jesus walked by, seizing the opportunity, the darkness at first pounced lightly. Then, once upon him, not wasting a second, the darkness had lunged for the kill, putting its death grip around Jesus' mind. The nameless darkness, no longer timid, then arrogantly voiced its identity in one word.

FEAR.

Tightening its deadly grip, intent upon dispelling totally any remaining light within Jesus, it began to singsong its chant of lies. "You also will die, Jesus. All that you have accomplished in the past has been for nothing. No one really believes in you. Take a look around…a very good look. What do your eyes behold, Jesus? What now surrounds you? The DEAD! The only truth is what you can *see*. Be assured, your soul *is* mine, reserved for hell, and you *will* rot in the grave that awaits you, Jesus.

Assaulted by fear, Jesus' feet stumbled for the briefest of moments. His mind in torment, it had triggered the troubled soul of his humanness. His body and emotions had responded. Not speaking the fear aloud, silently, Jesus wept.

As the tears sprang from his eyes and coursed down his face, the Jews that were leading him the way had immediately noticed. Taken aback by the display of emotions from Jesus, they had mistakenly assumed and marveled aloud to one another that Jesus must have loved Lazarus very much to be crying over his death! Some of them had continued, questioning aloud in wonder, saying that it would seem that a man that had been able to open blinded eyes surely could have kept Lazarus from dying.

As those around him were speaking, Jesus, upon hearing their words, became stirred in his spirit. Their words, unknowingly to them, had pierced through the darkness of fear that had temporarily blinded his own eyes to the spiritual truth of the situation. His heavenly Father was a Father of light, *never* darkness!

Cutting as sharply as a double-edged sword, dividing the light from the darkness, the truth from the lies, another remembrance of a promise of his heavenly Father had surged within him. For his heavenly Father, long ago in the endless past, had promised him faithfully that upon his son's death, he would *not* leave his soul in hell, nor would he allow his son's body to experience corruption while in the grave.

Not even having to hear a word spoken from the mouth of Jesus, the darkness of fear cringed, pulling away from the light of the truth which had once again begun, in full splendor, to shine forth from within Jesus. Hating the light, and rebuked by exposure, the fear silently slithered away in defeat.

With newly-opened eyes, Jesus found himself standing in front of, and facing, the stone that barred the entrance to the cave wherein Lazarus lay buried. He ordered the stone removed from the entrance.

Upon hearing Jesus' command, thinking only of the stench that would surely emanate from the cave once the stone became removed, Martha had asked if such an order would be wise.

Jesus, once again in full command of the situation, had patiently reminded her that he had told her earlier if she would believe, she would see the glory of God.

Proceeding with Jesus' directive, with much heaving and gasping, a group of male mourners began the task of moving aside the great stone preventing entrance into the sepulcher wherein Lazarus lay entombed. Finally, the stone rolled away, and those nearby felt the musty air within the tomb escape. A shaft of sunlight shone upon the tomb's entrance, piercing the dark and dank air as it now flowed forth from the tomb's interior, giving spotlight to the tiny particles of dust swirling and dancing within its light as they made their escape.

Having learned his lesson well, refusing to look again at natural appearances, Jesus lifted his eyes upward to his heavenly Father. Thankfully, so as to remind those that were with him of the source of his strength and power, and also that they would know and believe in his Father who had sent him, he had gratefully acknowledged that, as always, he had heard from his Father. And, as always, his Father had heard him.

Speaking the truth of his faith in his Father, the evidence not yet apparent, he had then spoken loudly and clearly, commanding Lazarus to come forth out the sepulcher.

And Lazarus, who had been dead, came out, his hands and feet still wrapped in grave clothes, with even his face still covered up. Triumphantly, knowing in whom he had believed, Jesus had commanded those nearby to unwrap Lazarus. Standing full in stature and confidence, Jesus made certain all would clearly *see*...love *never* fails...and love had lifted and set Lazarus free.

* * *

"Now that we know what we have—Jesus, this great High Priest with ready access to God—let's not let it slip through our fingers. We don't have a priest who is out of touch with our reality. He's been through weakness and testing, experienced it all—all but the sin. So let's walk right up to him and get what he is so ready to give. Take the mercy, accept the help.

Every high priest selected to represent men and women before God and offer sacrifices for their sins should be able to deal gently with their failings, since he knows what it's like from his own experience. But that also means that he has to offer sacrifices for his own sins as well as the people's.

No one elects himself to this honored position. He's called to it by God, as Aaron was. Neither did Christ presume to set himself up as high priest, but was set apart by the One who said, 'You're my son; today I celebrate you!' In another place God declares, 'You're a priest forever in the royal order of Melchizedek.'

While he lived on earth, anticipating death, Jesus cried out in pain and wept in sorrow as he offered up priestly prayers to God. Because he honored God, God answered him. Though he was God's Son, he learned trusting-obedience by what he suffered, just as we do. Then, having arrived at the full stature of his maturity and having been announced by God as high priest in the order of Melchizedek, he became the source of eternal salvation to all who believingly obey him."[14]

---

[14] Hebrews 4:14–5:10 (The Message)

CHAPTER 12

And it came to pass after these things, that God did tempt Abraham, and said unto him, Abraham: and he said, Behold, here I am.

And he said, Take now thy son, thine only son Isaac, whom thou lovest, and get thee into the land of Moriah; and offer him there for a burnt offering upon one of the mountains which I will tell thee of.

And Abraham rose up early in the morning, and saddled his ass, and took two of his young men with him, and Isaac his son, and clave the wood for the burnt offering, and rose up, and went unto the place of which God had told him.

Then on the third day Abraham lifted up his eyes, and saw the place afar off.

And Abraham said unto his young men, Abide ye here with the ass; and I and the lad will go yonder and worship, and come again unto you.

And Abraham took the wood of the burnt offering, and laid it upon Isaac his son; and he took the fire in his hand, and a knife; and they went both of them together.

And Isaac spake unto Abraham his father, and said, My father: and he said, Here am I, my son. And he said, Behold the fire and the wood: but where is the lamb for a burnt offering?

And Abraham said, My son, God will provide himself a lamb for a burnt offering: so they went both of them together.

And they came to the place which God had told him of; and Abraham built an altar there, and laid the wood in order, and bound Isaac his son, and laid him on the altar upon the wood.

And Abraham stretched forth his hand, and took the knife to slay his son.

And the angel of the Lord called unto him out of heaven, and said, Abraham, Abraham: and he said, Here am I.

And he said, Lay not thine hand upon the lad, neither do thou any thing unto him: for now I know that thou fearest God, seeing thou hast not withheld thy son, thine only son from me.

And Abraham lifted up his eyes, and looked, and behold behind him a ram caught in a thicket by his horns: and Abraham went and took the ram, and offered him up for a burnt offering in the stead of his son.

And Abraham called the name of the place Jehovah-jireh: as it is said to this day, In the mount of the Lord it shall be seen.

—Genesis 22:1–14

THE LAMB

The encumbered donkey brayed loudly, protesting at the hard tug of the reins attempting to coerce him into progressing at a more expeditious pace. Weary of the tedious journey and his heavily burdened back, the donkey rebelliously pulled firmly against the reins which bridled him. Lowering his long-eared shaggy head and digging his stalwart hooves deep into the hot sand, he stubbornly refused to obey his master's bidding.

Walking abreast of the defiant beast of burden, Abraham sighed deeply. He relaxed the reins held within his right hand, concluding that to expend any further effort at compelling the donkey into further motion would only result in futility. Instead, using his unoccupied hand to shade and shield his eyes, Abraham glanced upward, squinting into the distance. Under the glare of the blazing mid-morning sun, he briefly surveyed the remote horizon.

The white-haired patriarch was completely unfamiliar with the terrain he now surveyed. Having departed from the land of Beersheba, for the past three days he had traversed over forty miles into this foreign land known as Moriah, land which consisted of an entire mountainous terrain that stretched in a north-south direction amidst the desert's edge in which he now stood. From the onset of this excursion, knowing only the general direction he was to travel, he had not known specifically when or where the journey would conclude. He was traveling entirely by faith he would know the precise destination when he sighted it.

As his eyes continued to sweep the pale-blue and cloudless mid-morning horizon surrounding him, his scrutiny suddenly beheld a certain mountaintop several miles farther ahead in the distance. Abraham noted a distinctive difference in the mountain due to a solitary thick cloud formation encircling its peak. Instantly, he perceived his pilgrimage was nearing a conclusion.

Dropping his arm and his gaze, he transferred the reins to his left hand and turned to face the small group following closely behind on foot, accompanying him on this expedition. The group consisted of his only son, Isaac, who was but a lad, and two other young men, Eliezer and Ishmael, who were of the company of his family's faithful servants.

Isaac looked up at his father expectantly, his youthful eyes full of love and trust. Abraham smiled at his son and stepping forward, he reached out and drew Isaac close, affectionately encircling his arms around the boy's slender shoulders. Leaning his aged head down, he rested his leathered and worn cheek against the black and silky softness of his son's curly-topped head. He closed his eyes to fleetingly bask in the love and trust he had observed in his son's countenance.

Abraham's smile abruptly faded from his weathered face, replaced with solemnity. Resisting the tears beginning to form behind his thin eyelids, he swallowed hard. Blinking rapidly, he gently pulled away but kept a single hand on Isaac's shoulder. Lifting his gaze, he looked beyond Isaac as he held out his left hand to relinquish the reins of the bridled donkey to Ishmael, the nearest of the two servants who stood close by.

Addressing both Eliezer and Ishmael, Abraham directed, "Remove the pack and unsaddle the beast. There will be no further need of him at this time. Pitch the tent, for it is here we will set up our campsite." Eliezer and Ishmael promptly began as instructed.

A task in which they were all well accustomed, it was an ordinary directive familiar to them, for they were "sand-dwellers," a people who lived a semi-nomadic form of life. Not dwelling in permanently settled communities, their prevalent way of life consisted of wandering in the desert wilderness, living in tents and moving with their herds from oasis to oasis.

Gazing down at his son once again, his smile reappeared, etching deeper grooves into Abraham's already worn face. Fondly, he said to Isaac, "You may assist, my son. When they have finished unpacking the supplies, I will need you to tend to the animal."

Ishmael immediately tethered the donkey to a small stake of wood he drove into the desert sand, and then all began the tasks necessary to set-up their temporary encampment. While Abraham set forth with traversing the base of the nearby mountain range to gather tinder and kindling necessary to build and start a small fire, Ishmael and Eliezer busied themselves with relieving the donkey of his burden.

They first removed water contained in tightly-tied animal skins which hung straddling both flanks of the donkey's girth, carefully placing them aside. Reaching underneath the donkey to untie the ropes of goat hair which snugly confined his encumbrance, they proceeded unloading the remaining array of supplies heaped upon the beast: dried figs and cakes of wheat bread stuffed with goat's cheese and wrapped within clean linen cloths, a folded tent of goat's hair cloth having wooden pegs and poles firmly encased within the midst, rolled-up hand-woven rugs of brightly colored wool, and a numerous assortment of leather bags and pouches filled with utensils and sundry provisions, beneath which was a bundle of split wood brought to build the fire for a burnt offering of worship. Lastly, they removed the blanket saddle of layered felt, straw, and haircloth.

Concentrating upon the next immediate task at hand, Eliezer and Ishmael selected the tent which consisted of long, tightly-wound strips of black goat's hair cloth, each section approximately six feet wide, jointly woven together. Reaching into the folds of the center, they first removed all wooden pegs and poles placed within the midst of the folded cloth, laying them temporarily aside. Grasping each end of the folded tent, together, they lifted its hefty bulk. Walking it a measurable distance beyond to lower it, they unfolded the tent completely, spreading it out evenly upon the desert floor.

Eliezer and Ishmael returned to the supply stash to acquire a mallet, various lengths of goat hair ropes, and then to also retrieve all wooden pegs and poles earlier placed aside.

Starting with a short end, Eliezer began placing pegs on the ground in alignment with each leather-thong loop sewn in intervals along the border edges of the tent. Advancing around three edges, omitting the last long length of border edge, Eliezer then fetched the mallet. Working his way back, he began the task of driving each rough wooden peg deep into the sand.

As Eliezer drove each peg, Ishmael followed behind. Using the shorter ropes of goat hair, to each peg he tied and attached a corresponding border-edged leather loop. After completing all three border edges, both Ishmael and Eliezer began erecting the tent. Inserting a wooden pole inside both the mid-center and outer border edge, they repeated the process within each subsequent end, leaving the opposite long edge of the tent open.

Fastening longer ropes to the border-edged loops of the open tent end, again they once more tied and looped the loose free ends to additional pegs. As they pulled and stretched taut each rope one-by-one, driving its attached peg into the sand, the tent became firmly anchored when completed.

To uniformly cover the ground underneath the tent's taut canopy, they gathered and unrolled a portion of the woolen rugs. Stacking the remaining rugs near an inside end pole, they would later unfurl them in the evening to provide warmth and cover from the desert's chilly night air. Ishmael and Eliezer collected and organized the remaining supplies, storing them alongside the remaining rugs beneath the shelter.

As the camp was set in order, Isaac meanwhile located a small wooden stand used as support for a leather receptacle that, combined, served as a watering trough. Putting both under his left arm and slinging a filled waterskin over his right shoulder, he hauled them across the campsite to the tethered donkey.

Using his right hand, he grabbed the stand and receptacle from under his left arm, positioning them onto the ground. Firmly planting the wooden stand upon the sweltering desert sand, he then placed the leather receptacle on top of the wooden stand, creating the trough. Removing the waterskin sling from his shoulder and loosening the leather cords gathered at the top, he positioned it above the trough. Mindful not to allow a drop of water to splash over, for it was an extremely precious staple, he allowed the water to slowly pour into the trough.

The donkey lowered his head and immediately began to greedily gulp dry the contents. The donkey's thirst slated, Isaac collected the trough and waterskin. Carrying all items, he returned to the tent and dutifully stored the trough to the supply area and slung the empty waterskin atop a supporting end pole. Wiping his sweaty brow with the sleeve of his tunic, he then scurried to sit under the welcoming shadow of the tent's canopy, thankful to have a means of relief from the sun's blisteringly hot rays.

Mid-day approaching, the tent pitched, and camp set in order, the young servants also shortly joined Isaac in acquiring alleviation from the scorching heat. Abraham, in the meantime, had returned to the camp and built a small fire along the outward perimeter. He now continued to equip himself for the final trek in reaching the distant mountain peak.

Rummaging through the supplies, he found a lengthy piece of hemp rope, and loosely coiled it, tossing it around his neck. From within a sack of various utensils, he located a sheathed, short-bladed dagger. Inserting it under the leather stringed waistband of his long, loose tunic, he placed it securely at his side.

Departing from the shade of the tent, Abraham stepped over to the bundle of wood which he had personally cut and split. Brought for the burnt offering of worship, it was approximately three feet long by two feet wide, tied at each end with goats-hair rope. Sighting a long, straight length of green wood that he had intentionally placed in the bundle prior to their beginning departure, he extracted it and put it aside, apart from the stack.

Grabbing the coil of rope and lifting it from around his neck, he unwound the loops and stooping down, stretched its long length upon the ground. Picking up the bundle of wood, he placed it across the middle of the length of rope, tying the ends firmly into a knot, midway around its bulk. Then, on each end of the length of rope which now remained, he formed a small loop just about the width of his hand, knotting each end's loop separately with a slipknot.

Retrieving the stick of green wood he had set aside, Abraham again returned to his supplies and searched among them until he came upon a small leather pouch. Loosening the strings of the pouch, he opened it and drew out several oil-soaked rags. Methodically, he began to wrap the oily rags carefully around one end of the green stick of wood, then fastened them in place with a long, narrow strip of the fabric. Striding to the fire he had kindled earlier, he nudged the wrapped end of the stick into the flames, causing the oil-soaked fabric to ignite.

All tasks of his preparations now completed, Abraham called out for Isaac but heard not a reply. Glancing backward, toward the tent, he espied Isaac dozing underneath the shade of the tent canopy, comfortably curled on his side, his head atop a solitary rolled-up rug.

Propping the lighted torch at the edge of the campfire, Abraham went to arouse his son from sleep. Bending down slightly, ever so gently, he lightly shook Isaac's shoulder.

"Isaac, my son, come. I have need of you for we must now continue with our travel."

Isaac half-opened his eyes, not quite fully awake. His dark hair tousled and damply clinging to his perspiring brow, he slightly raised his head and with heavily-lidded eyes caught a disoriented glance of his father's face. It was a few seconds before he realized what his father had spoken. But as soon as his sleepy mind apprehended the words, he startled to alertness. Always eager to please his father, he scrambled to his feet.

"I am ready, Father," he earnestly stated. "What may I do to help you?"

Solemnly, Abraham replied, "Come with me, my son."

Grasping Isaac by the hand, he led him to the bundle of wood bound with rope. Halting, Abraham turned to face his son. Bringing his large and gnarled hands together, Isaac's small and smooth hand clutched and engulfed within them, he momentarily held his son's hand next to his chest, close to his heart. Tenderly releasing Isaac's hand, Abraham softly instructed his son, "I will need you to turn around and stretch out your arms wide." Without hesitation, Isaac did as his father requested.

As Isaac stood with his back facing his father, arms outstretched wide, Abraham bent over and lifted the bundle of wood. Using his right hand to prop and support the wood against the middle of Isaac's back, with his left hand, he caught one end of the dangling rope and put Isaac's left hand through the circular loop. Continuing to bring the loop up the length of Isaac's arm until it reached the boy's shoulder, he then adjusted and pulled the slipknot snug.

Transferring the support of the bundle of wood now to his left hand, using the dangling looped-end of rope that remained, Abraham repeated the same process on Isaac's right arm.

And so it was, with his arms outstretched wide, Isaac received the burden of wood his father laid upon him.

Abraham stepped around to peer down at his son and asked, "Will it be too much of a burden, son?"

Lowering his arms, Isaac hooked his thumbs under the loops of rope that now circumferenced about his shoulders. Gazing up intently into his father's face, Isaac confidently replied, "I am able, Father."

As Abraham looked down at his son, his paternal heart seemed to catch in his throat. Hastily, so that his son could not observe his tumultuous emotions, Abraham turned to look away from the purity of his son's innocent, upturned face.

Determined not to give in to his raging emotions, instead, he stepped the distance to the campfire, stooped to retrieve the lighted torch propped on the edge, then again stood upright. Looking ahead, he set his face toward the distant mount of Moriah, resolving to conclude the excursion as soon as possible.

Pivoting slightly and pointing to the highest mountain peak in the distance, he addressed Eliezer and Ishmael, "It will not be necessary for you young men to accompany me any farther. I shall have you remain here. The lad and I will return after we have gone yonder to worship."

Torch in hand, Abraham nodded at his son. Isaac nodded in return, adjusting the weight of the burden upon his back. Together, Father and son began to walk the final trek of their passage to reach the site of their worship.

Shortening his stride for Isaac's sake, the day's afternoon was almost depleted when they finally neared the mountain peak. As the hours had passed, neither Father nor son spoke during their trek of the desert's expanse, both lost in their own separate thoughts. The searing heat had not permitted the luxury of exhausting their energy on conversation.

Abraham had spent the time pondering the past events of his life. From the time of his birth to the present, he pondered how very extraordinary was his existence and how much the Lord God Jehovah had totally transformed every aspect of his life.

* * *

Originally named Abram at birth, he had been born a Mesopotamian in the city of Ur of the Chaldees. There he lived with his father and brothers until manhood. It was in Mesopotamia he met and married his beautiful wife, Sarai.

While in Mesopotamia, Abram and his entire family followed the custom of the land by worshipping the innumerable idols common to the populace. But at age seventy-five, Abram's life drastically changed when the living God, Jehovah, spoke to him, directing Abram to depart from the land of dead idols and to worship Jehovah exclusively. Abram was to take his wife, leave the land of Mesopotamia, and go to a land unknown to him, a land Jehovah would guide him to with the promise of great blessing.

Abram obeyed the Lord God Jehovah's voice and, indeed, the Lord was faithful to his word. During the subsequent twenty-four years, Abram's life had spilled to overflowing with possession of enormous wealth in gold, silver, servants, land, cattle, flocks, and prestige. It had been more than any man could desire.

But for one detail.

When Abram had departed from Mesopotamia, the Lord had also sworn with an everlasting covenant he made to Abram, that Sarai and Abram would have many descendants. So many, in fact, their descendants would outnumber the stars in heaven.

Yet twenty-four years had elapsed while dwelling in the new land, and Abram and his wife, Sarai, remained childless. By then, both had advanced well beyond the age of child-bearing years.

It was after the twenty-four years had elapsed, at Abram's age of ninety-nine, that the Lord had appeared to Abram to remind and reassure him he had promised many descendants to them and he, the Lord, did not go back on his word. Abram and Sarai could expect a child born to them within the following year. The child would be a son, whose name they would call Isaac, meaning "laughter." And with their prospective son Isaac, the Lord would also establish an everlasting covenant, as well as with Isaac's descendants. Of that Abram could be confident.

To further enforce and establish his former vow to them, the Lord also told Abram that he would change their names. The Lord had changed Abram's name to "Abraham," meaning "father of a multitude," and Sarai's name to "Sarah," meaning "mother of princes."

From that day forth, every time Abraham and his wife called each other by their new names, it had reminded them of the Lord's vow made to them. It also prompted them not to consider they were both past the age of child-bearing years, but to rely on the faithfulness of the Lord's pledge to them, no matter what the circumstances appeared. They both knew, from their past experiences since knowing the Lord, the Lord was not slack concerning his promises.

And so it happened, within a year from the Lord's appearance to Abraham to remind him of the pledge, Sarah had conceived and given birth to their promised son, Isaac.

Abraham could not help but beam with delight as he now remembered that jubilant day. Abraham and Sarah's joy had then known no constraint! In the pursuant years which had followed, they had never ceased to praise and magnify the Lord for bringing the miracle of Isaac into their lives.

His thoughts revolving again back to the present, Abraham's expression became clouded with an air of somberness as he continued to reflect.

Contrary to the joyful routine of life in which Abraham was now accustomed, only days before, unexpectedly, the Lord had called unto Abraham with a severe request. He had asked Abraham to take his only son, his cherished Isaac, go to the land of Moriah to a certain location which the Lord would show him, and there take the life of his son. He was to thereupon sacrifice Isaac as a burnt offering of worship to the Lord.

Abraham had not spoken a word of the Lord's supplication to anyone. For who would understand? Abraham himself could not conceive in his own mind why the Lord would ask him to make such a sacrifice. The Lord had asked him to take the life of his son, and with his own hands!

On that day of the Lord's petition, overwhelmed by many thoughts of fear and doubt, Abraham began to question himself. *Have I done something to displease the Lord? Will I have the courage to perform what the Lord has requested of me? If Isaac asks any questions during the journey, how will I answer? According to the traditions the Lord has taught me, why has the Lord asked me to offer my son, instead of a lamb, for a burnt offering?*

That entire day Abraham anxiously pondered in his heart and mind these questions. Upon that night of the Lord's appeal, Abraham had slept fitfully, wrestling with the thoughts of his tortured mind and emotions. Nevertheless, as the dawning light rays of daybreak awakened him from his erratic rest, he knew he had no choice but to obey the Lord's request. For whatever reason that the Lord was asking him to do such a thing, to honor the Lord, Abraham would be obedient.

For Abraham had remembered something late into the night of his painful agonizing. Something which had ultimately released him to make the decision he would obey the Lord's entreaty.

When the Lord had long ago visited him to foretell him of Isaac's upcoming birth, and that his covenant of blessing with Abraham would also perpetually extend to Isaac, including Isaac's descendants,

Abraham knew the Lord would never go back on his word; his words were immutable.

When those words of the Lord's vow returned to his remembrance on that night, it was then that Abraham had made his peace with the Lord's request. Due to the Lord's everlasting covenant established with Abraham and Isaac, Abraham would not withhold his only son of promise from God.

Yes, he would sacrifice his only son's life and offer Isaac's lifeless body back to the one who had originally given him life. But he would also await the Lord to then resurrect Isaac from the dead and restore his life back unto him. Abraham fully believed and expected the Lord to be faithful to the covenant he had long ago made. *For of one thing I am persuaded and have no doubt,* Abraham had reckoned, *the Lord God Jehovah is the God of miracles.*

It was due to his assurance and belief in the integrity of the Lord and his covenant with him that Abraham had made the statement he did to his two faithful servants before he and Isaac had left on their journey to the mount, "The lad and I *will* return after we have gone yonder to worship."

* * *

Abraham and Isaac's progress had slowed considerably as they trudged upward through the thick underbrush on the craggy slope of the mountain, having almost reached its peak. The higher altitude and physical exertion required for the ascent was causing them both to have to pause at intervals to catch their breath.

Abraham stopped to wipe his brow with his left hand, his other hand occupied with carrying the lighted torch. Isaac came to a halt also, standing close behind his father. Isaac's voice interrupted the lengthy silence that had been their companion.

"Father?" Isaac questioned.

With his eyes widened below his raised, bushy eyebrows, Abraham turned to cast a quizzical look at Isaac as he replied, "Yes, my son?"

"Father, I've been thinking." Abraham noted the serious puzzlement in Isaac's voice as he continued, "We have the wood and the
fire for the burnt offering…" Isaac paused, his forehead furrowed in
studious thought about the customary observance of their worship.
"But where is the lamb?"

Abraham's heart felt as if it had stilled within his chest. He
could hear the blood as it rushed to his head, filling his ears with its
pulsing sound.

Taken aback by Isaac's question, Abraham promptly turned
away from his son. Casting his eyes heavenward, he quietly beseeched
the Lord. His mind could not imagine how he could answer with
any manner of speech, nor with what words. Yet as if from a distance, from deep within the abundance of his heart, he heard his own
mouth audibly speak a response. "God will provide himself a lamb,
my son."

Indicating it was time to resume their quest, Abraham stepped
forward. Isaac quietly followed his father, and together, they began
the conclusion of their pilgrimage.

Soon arriving at the mount's summit, Abraham stopped to prop
the torch upright at the edge of a steep mountain crag, then turned
about to unencumber his son from the burden of wood he had com-
pliantly transported. Slackening the rope's slipknots upon Isaac's
shoulders, he slowly pulled the loosened slipknots down the length
of Isaac's arms, allowing the fettered wood to descend to the ground.

Freed from his burden, Isaac stretched and rotated his limbs,
enjoying the abandon of restraint. To ease his back, he leaned against
a large imposing boulder and curiously watched as his father spared
not a moment's rest in proceeding to build an altar.

Kneeling on one knee, Abraham untied and freed all ropes from
the unfettered wood's girth, leaving them lay where they fell once
untied. Pushing himself again to an upright position, he began the
task of building and forming the altar upon which to perform the
ceremonial burnt offering.

Systematically, he began collecting and mounding large loose
stones upon an area base several feet in length and width. Next, he
selected the now unfettered wood bundle, arranging the split pieces

atop the altar stones. Lastly, he gathered tinder and kindling from the area underbrush, placing it amongst the stone gaps and the larger wood pieces.

Finishing the preparation of the altar, he bent forward to grasp a short length of freed rope he had laid on the ground when loosed from the bundle. Resuming full stance, he hesitated briefly in an attempt to restrain his emotions. His heart still pounding clamorously within his chest, resolutely, he advanced toward his son.

Isaac looked up questioningly into his father's face. Abraham returned the gaze, silently imploring his son for understanding. Then breaking his gaze, he looked down to reach out and grasp Isaac's hands. Slowly, he brought them together, placing one atop the other. Using the length of rope he had fetched, he wound it snugly around his son's thin wrists, binding them securely.

Again, kneeling on one knee, Abraham retrieved the last short length of rope and also securely bound his son's dusty ankles.

Immersed in his father's silence, Isaac now comprehended.

Still kneeling, placing one arm behind his son's knees and the other encircling his son's back, Abraham lifted Isaac off the ground, gathering his treasured son up into his arms. For but an instant, Abraham longingly held Isaac near to himself, close to his thumping heart, burying his bearded face next to the smoothness of Isaac's youthful cheek. And as he wavered in that instant of eternity, a great trembling took hold of his aged body, and he knew he must surrender his son immediately, or he would have his former resolve crumble in defeat.

Yielding from the temptation to forever embrace and cling to Isaac, instead, in absolute submission to only the Lord's will, Abraham tenderly laid his son down upon the altar he had created, placing his son's back against the roughly hewn wood.

Without a struggle, nor having spoken a word in protest, in unity with his father, Isaac's limp body conveyed he would surrender his life into his father's hands.

Standing above him, Abraham looked down upon his beloved son and saw that Isaac had tightly squeezed his eyes shut.

Clutching the handle of the sheathed dagger which rested securely under the waistband of his tunic, Abraham swiftly drew it out from within its leather encasement. Drawing himself to full height, he raised the honed knife up as far as he could reach, now clasping it with both hands, prepared to quickly plunge the knife into his son's heart. It seemed as if the very earth held its breath, suspending all activity in quiet reverence to pay homage to the deed of submission Abraham was about to perpetrate.

"Abraham, Abraham!" the voice thundered, calling unto him from out of the stilled heavens.

Startled, Abraham raised his face upward, seeking the voice. "Yes? I am here."

"Lay not your hand upon the lad, neither do you any harm to him. For now I know your love for me, seeing you would not withhold your only son from me."

Abraham thought his heart was going to burst with joy. He closed his eyes and allowed the tears that sprang within them to stream down the wizened and leathery grooves of his face. Sinking to his knees, opening his eyes to look through the blur of tears, he replaced the knife back into its sheath.

Bending over to draw Isaac into his trembling arms, he again closed his eyes as he rocked back and forth, all the while holding his precious son in a hard embrace, his chest now heaving with the greatness of his sobs as he permitted his emotions to run their fragile course.

Finally, his sobs abated, and his heart settled to a calmer beat. Releasing his grip from Isaac, he pushed himself back to behold his son and realized he had not yet detached the ropes which still constrained his son. Hurriedly, he untied the cords from Isaac's hands and feet, setting him free.

Isaac flung his freed arms around his father's neck and once again Abraham locked his son in a tight embrace. Joyously and with total abandon, Abraham smothered his son with kisses of ecstatic thankfulness.

The elated celebration suddenly became unexpectedly interrupted by a distracting commotion from behind. Glancing around,

Abraham beheld a mature male lamb caught by his horns in the mount's thick underbrush. At first puzzled, comprehension then flooded his mind. *The burnt offering! The Lord has miraculously provided the customary lamb as a substitute for Isaac!*

Tarrying not a moment, he made his way through the dense brush to the entangled ram. Disengaging the dagger from its sheath, with confident accuracy, he thrust the sharp knife into the snared animal, providing the ram a swift death. Once assured all life had drained from the ram, he lifted and placed the lifeless carcass upon the fashioned altar of wood.

Advancing to the lighted torch which still remained propped against the mountain crag, Abraham took it into his hand and returning, immersed the flaming torch into the dry tinder and wood of the altar. First smoldering, the dry materials crackled and popped as the flame took hold before then erupting into a blast of fervent combustion, the blaze leaping heavenward. The carcass of the ram promptly became smothered with the thick smoke and fiery flames of the ceremonial altar.

Thus, the ceremony of worship to the Lord became accomplished and completed as Abraham offered the ram's blazing consummation unto the Lord as a substitute in the stead of his son, Isaac.

And from that day forth, Abraham called the mount of Moriah Jehovah-Jireh, meaning "the Lord will provide." For on the mount of Moriah, Abraham had miraculously witnessed the Lord provide a lamb of sacrifice.

And so it is said to this day, "In the mount of the Lord it shall be seen."

Indeed, the Lord will provide.

* * *

The few witnesses who still lingered and heard him could not fathom from where he mustered the strength to cry out.

His anguished voice echoed off the neighboring mountains as he turned his battered and blood-crusted face upward and called out with a loud voice to him who resided in the now darkened and silent heavens.

"My God, my God! Why have you forsaken me?"

It seemed as if all of creation held its breath, suspending activity to await a response as his voice reverberated into the darkened sky.

In the land known as Moriah, land which consisted of all the mountains of the Jerusalem area, high atop a certain mountain peak, the Father's only begotten Son hung suspended, nailed by his sinewy wrists and dusty feet to a rugged wooden cross.

Always eager to please his father, with his arms outstretched wide, he had received the burden of wood his father had laid upon him. Without a struggle, nor having spoken a word in protest, in unity with his father, his limp body conveyed he would surrender his life into the hands of the Roman soldiers.

Six hours he hung nailed to the wood of the cross, enduring tormenting pain and suffering beyond mortal comprehension.

As his father witnessed from the heavens the passing of the first three hours, a great trembling took hold of his ancient body, for he longed to rescue his treasured Son and gather him up into his arms, holding him near to himself.

And as he wavered in that instant of eternity, he knew he too must surrender. Immediately, totally, and completely.

And so, knowing that to yield to the temptation to forever embrace and cling to his Son would revoke and annul this ultimate sacrifice, for the final three hours, his father had turned to look away.

The luminant glory of his face now averted, a resulting darkness apprehended and covered the whole land. Darkness and silence.

Immersed in his father's silence, Jesus now comprehended.

Determined to not yield to his raging emotions, his father had set his face toward the objective of offering his Son as the ultimate provisional sacrifice.

Mankind's redemption.

For just as in the days of Abraham when he had provided a ram as a substitute for the sacrifice of Isaac to spare his life, it was now that he had provided his Son, Jesus, as a substitute to redeem all mankind who would acknowledge him as the sacrifice substituted to spare *their* lives. What he had originally asked Abraham to perform, he himself had now done. He had offered *his* only begotten Son.

His Lamb.

Now, as the remaining three hours had passed in vast darkness and stillness, sensing the end of his life nearing, his Son had broken the silence. Hearing the voiced question shouted and reverberating through the heavens, his father instantly turned back to face his Son.

From the heavens above, looking down upon his beloved Son, he saw that Jesus had tightly squeezed his eyes shut.

Without further detainment, his father radiated his almighty, divine presence, the luminance of his glory returning. The gross darkness covering the whole land dissipated, the darkened sky majestically acclaimed the return of his father's countenance by illuminating the heavens with bolted flashes of lightning; the earth quaked, rocks split, tombs opened, and dead bodies rose from graves.

Instantaneously, Jesus responded by crying out with a loud voice, acknowledging his father's returned presence. Reassured now, into his father's hands he gratefully committed himself, dismissing his spirit and soul. The Lamb of God had concluded the surrender and sacrificing of his life, leaving his now lifeless body upon the altar of wood.

It was finished.

And so it was, from that day forth, on the mount of Moriah, the world would forevermore proclaim having miraculously witnessed the Lord provide the Lamb, a performance of provision by the Lord of that which had long ago been promised and spoken, "In the mount of the Lord it shall be seen."

Indeed, the Lord had provided.

* * *

The next day John seeth Jesus coming unto him, and saith, Behold the Lamb of God, which taketh away the sin of the world.[15]

---

[15] John 1:29

ABOUT THE AUTHOR

Becoming a born-again Christian at the age of twenty-nine, with no previous church background or upbringing, Ms. Miller discovered that in reading her Bible, there were many scriptures that seemed to bring to her mind more questions than answers. After nearly a decade of wondering, she finally took to heart the advice the Bible provided in 2 Timothy 2:15 and personally began to immerse herself in a quest to, "study to shew thyself approved unto God." For nearly forty years now, it has remained her passion to continually study and pass on to others the beauty of the scriptures and the answers they contain. Weaving the answers into story form has provided one way for her to do so. Having a degree in surgical technology, Ms. Miller is now retired from her occupation as a surgical nurse and resides in Oklahoma. She is a recent graduate of Greenwood Bible College. Pastimes include instructing and facilitating small group Bible studies, gourmet cooking, knitting, painting, and crafting.

CPSIA information can be obtained
at www.ICGtesting.com
Printed in the USA
LVHW020608010821
694125LV00004B/433